Ever Feel Like an Outsider?

Ruth

How an
Outsider
Gained
God's
Favor

Ever Feel Like an Outsider?

How an
Outsider
Gained
God's
Favor

Harry L. Brewer

WINEPRESS WP PUBLISHING

© 2001 by Harry L. Brewer. All rights reserved

Printed in the United States of America

Packaged by WinePress Publishing, PO Box 428, Enumclaw, WA 98022. The views expressed or implied in this work do not necessarily reflect those of WinePress Publishing. Ultimate design, content, and editorial accuracy of this work are the responsibilities of the author.

No part of this publication may be reproduced, stored in a retrieval system, or transmitted in any way by any means—electronic, mechanical, photocopy, recording, or otherwise—without the prior permission of the copyright holder, except as provided by USA copyright law.

Unless otherwise noted all scriptures are taken from the Holy Bible, New International Version, Copyright © 1973, 1978, 1984 by the International Bible Society. Used by permission of Zondervan Publishing House. The "NIV" and "New International Version" trademarks are registered in the United States Patent and Trademark Office by International Bible Society.

ISBN 1-57921-327-8
Library of Congress Catalog Card Number: 00-108097

*To my grandchildren,
Gaige, Adrianna, Portia, Savannah, Alyssa, Darianne, and Tiana.
May you grow up as people who follow God
and gain His favor.*

Acknowledgments

The significance of this book lies in the understanding of Scripture, the principles for studying it and respect for one's personal relationship with God. These things are ingrained in me, because I learned them throughout my life from many people. I acknowledge educators, ministers, friends, and family for their contribution to my spiritual understanding and perceptions. I acknowledge work colleagues, too numerous to name, for their contribution to my life.

My study of Ruth was performed with rigor in the original Hebrew. I thank friends who contributed directly to this effort. Herschel Owens challenged the format and contributed to the current presentation. Edie Crytzer and my mother-in-law, Ernestine Schmidt, made editing and textual suggestions.

Special thanks is given to Rebecca Rogers who ferreted time from her demanding schedule to create the artwork. My home group also participated: Bill and Meryl Konrad, Harry and Joyce Gries, Mark and Catherine Ruben, and Molly Haberman.

Acknowledgments

My parents, Harry and Dorothy; my brother, Jerry; my children, Jeremy and Angela; and my wife, Holly, have offered encouragement and insight.

I am beholden to each of the above for their contribution to this effort.

Gratefully,
Harry L. Brewer
January 2001

Contents

Preface xi
Introduction xiii

1—The Consequences of Not Following God 17
2—The Decision to Follow God 33
3—The Actions of Following God 49
4—The Benefit of Following God 67
5—The Challenge of Following God 79
6—The Practice of Waiting with God 95
7—The Trial of Following God 103
8—The Blessings of Following God 117
9—Reflections on Ruth 129

Preface

Ruth was courageous. She endured the difficulties of a cross-cultural marriage, but within ten years her husband died. She was left a young, childless widow with her widowed mother-in-law.

In the face of tragedy she committed herself to her mother-in-law and to God. Within a few months her consistent, ethical behavior won the favor of a small, Jewish community and a prestigious blessing from God.

These events took place more than 3,000 years ago, yet she is a role model in synagogues and churches today. Her story is worth examining as a model for spiritual values.

The book of Ruth unfolds the story of a woman named Ruth, how she finds God is brought into His family and gains His favor. It is considered Holy Scripture, found in the Jewish Tenakh and in the Roman Catholic and Protestant Old Testaments. It is one of two or three books in Scripture named after a woman.

Many have written about this biblical book. It is a lovely romantic story. However, few have addressed in detail the spiritual truths exemplified in this book. I wrote this book to provide an easily understood, in-depth study of the book of Ruth. It follows the scriptural record verse by verse, sometimes phrase by phrase.

The scriptural passages quoted at the beginning of each chapter are from the New International Version® [NIV] of the Holy Bible translated by the International Bible Society. The scriptural quotes for each verse are interpreted by the author for detailed accuracy and insight into the specific passage. References to biblical passages outside of Ruth are also quoted from the New International Version®.

I have chosen to accept the book of Ruth as Scripture at face value and discuss its contents. If you are interested in examining the contents of Ruth, you have come to the right place—enjoy!

I write to encourage those who are interested in the spiritual truths found in the book of Ruth. They are applicable to all civilizations that endorse a God of justice and grace. I find them profound and appropriate in our modern society. It gives me pleasure to present my thoughts for your consideration.

INTRODUCTION

MODELS OF SPIRITUAL LEADERSHIP

A Personal Example

One of the finest men I know is a farmer who negotiates the sale of thousands of dollars of crops on a word and a handshake. He doesn't talk much about his faith, but he lives it honestly and consistently. His life exemplifies character in following God. I am grateful for his example and influence on my life.

Scriptural Examples

Scripture records the lives of hundreds of people. Many model character in following God. Few do it without straying or wavering.

Excellent Examples

Two excellent models are Joseph and Daniel. Joseph's life story is recorded from his youth until he dies at age 110. When he was a teenager Joseph's brothers sold him into slavery. At thirty he became second highest ruler in Egypt, next to Pharaoh. He forgave and rescued the family of his father and brothers from a seven-year famine. He followed God consistently throughout his life.

Introduction

As a teenager Daniel was taken captive to Babylon, where he spent the remainder of his life. Scripture records events of his life as a teenager, young man, adult, and venerated leader, with no wrong ever mentioned. He lived an exemplary life. Joseph and Daniel truly model character in following God.

Human Examples

Some scriptural personalities were great leaders but far from perfect. Take Abraham, Moses and King David. These great men made major mistakes. Abraham lied about his wife; Moses killed an Egyptian; and David had an adulterous affair and then had the woman's husband killed. Yet none of them persisted in doing wrong as a lifestyle.

These men repented to God and accepted the consequences of their wrongs. They continued to seek God, and He blessed them. Though imperfect, they still knew God, followed Him and led people in His ways. These men were spiritual and national leaders.

A Questionable Example

What about a man like Samson? He was great, until a woman caught his eye. Then he was in trouble. Every problem in his life could be traced to a woman. He led Israel for thirty years, yet never conquered a fundamental problem.

This problem ended his leadership and freedom. It led him to prison. Graciously God granted him a hero's victory to end his life. He showed some character and great weakness.

Only God can judge the heart. Yet God followers become apparent from their lifestyle. A godly man may stumble, but he will return to good. An ungodly man will return to what is wrong, because there is no intention in his heart to do what is good. It is always harder to do what is good than not. Those who follow God choose and sacrifice to do what is ethically right.

Ruth

The central character in the book of Ruth is a woman named Ruth, who finds God and follows His ways throughout her life. She did not write the book. It is what someone else saw in watching her life: a woman who demonstrated spiritual values.

Her behavior elicited the favor of a small Jewish community and God's blessing that assimilated her into the Jewish royal family. Her journey was fraught with tragedy, hardship and adversity. In everything she demonstrates commitment to God, His ethical ways and His people.

CHAPTER ONE

THE CONSEQUENCES OF NOT FOLLOWING GOD

INTRODUCTION

Chapter 1 Opening

Chapter 1 sets the historical background for our story in ancient Israel during the period of the judges. It also introduces a family that is key to the story. Unfortunately the father makes bad decisions that take the family away from the people of God. He and his sons die in a foreign land.

Biblical Text

> [1]In the days when the judges judged, there was a famine in the land, and a man from Bethlehem in Judah, he and his wife and two sons, went to live for a while in the land of Moab. [2]The man's name was Elimelech, and his wife's name was Naomi, and the names of his two sons were Mahlon and Kilion. They were Ephrathites from Bethlehem, Judah. And they went to the land of Moab and lived there.

> ³Now Elimelech, Naomi's husband, died, and she was left with her two sons. ⁴They took for themselves Moabite wives; the name of the one was Orpah and the name of the second was Ruth. After they had lived there about ten years, ⁵the two of them also died, Mahlon and Kilion; and Naomi was left without her two sons and her husband.
>
> —Ruth 1:1–5

Key Spiritual Principle: Not following God is detrimental to our lives

For believers, life consists of learning and following God's ways. Following God is the preferred lifestyle.

God's way is a difficult path to follow. It introduces more than the usual share of adversity and challenges. We may make suggestions to God to ease or improve our path, suggestions on what should happen in our lives or what He could do to help (in our opinion). God invariably brings us back to His plans and asks us to follow them.

Generally it's difficult for me to tell if God's way is better. I follow Him by faith, simply trusting that His way is better. Occasionally, in retrospect, I get a glimpse of what He has done. The results are always beyond anything I had considered.

Of course, we can refuse and follow our own desires. But God will not honor those activities. They generally have little value and lead us into trouble.

Our story gives a worst-case scenario. A man takes his family and leaves God's ways. The consequences are tragic.

THE SETTING

At the time of our story, Israel was in its infancy, struggling to establish itself as a nation. Law and order were controlled loosely. Men, families and communities took care of themselves and each

Ruth 1:1 In the days when the judges ruled, there was a famine in the land, and a man from Bethlehem in Judah, together with his wife and two sons, went to live for a while in the country of Moab.

other. They became the source of protection, strength and opportunity. Family and community are integral to this story.

The Historical Period (verse 1a)

> In the days when the judges judged,

Background

After Moses led the people of Israel out of Egypt, Joshua led them in the conquest of the "promised land." During Joshua's life the nation followed him and the ways of the Lord.

The generation that grew up after Joshua's death forgot the ways of Joshua and God. The people of Israel fell into a cycle:
1. They would fall away from the Lord
2. An enemy would conquer them
3. They would call to the Lord for help
4. The Lord would send a judge to lead and rescue them from their enemy
5. They would follow the Lord, and He would bless them

After a while, they would fall away from the Lord again. This cycle recurred for 300 years.

Our story is a microcosm of this cycle. Main characters leave God and His people. They encounter tragedy. Two return to God and His people. They follow the Lord, Who restores and blesses them.

Judges

The judges were God-chosen leaders who rescued Israel from her enemies and led the people in God's ways. They were prominent in Jewish history just after the time of Joshua. The scriptural book of Judges records the accounts of fourteen judges who rescued and led Israel, including Gideon, Deborah, Jephthah, and Samson.

The story of Ruth occurs during the period of the judges. The heritage of Boaz, a principal character introduced later, places our story around 1300 BC.

The Problem (verse 1b)

there was a famine in the land,

Our story begins with a problem—a famine. A famine is a natural event, in which the land does not yield crops. It imposes hard times on people's lives.

Metaphorically a famine can represent personal difficulties. We have a saying that uses a contrasting metaphor: "Into every life a little rain must fall." It means that everyone experiences hard times. However, difficulties are not necessarily the result of mistakes or wrong doings. In the book of Job, God permits Satan to inflict trials and suffering on Job to prove his devotion and faithfulness. In Job's case there is no wrong indicated for his problems.

From scriptural accounts and from our own personal experience, we learn that both spiritual and unspiritual people experience good and bad circumstances in their lives. The circumstances do not determine whether a person is spiritual or not. A person's response to the circumstances is what's important.

The famine came. Perhaps it was a test; perhaps just part of life on earth. In his book, *The Problem of Pain*, C. S. Lewis gives pain a purpose: to remind us that this is not heaven; there is something beyond this obstacle-ridden, terrestrial existence.

THE CHOICE

Life contains numerous events, opportunities and choices. Our responsibility is to follow God and make good ethical choices. In our story a man chooses to move his family from their own community and nation to another nation, from Israel to Moab.

The Family (verse 1c)

> and a man from Bethlehem in Judah, his wife and two sons,

This man has one of the finest heritages in Israel. He is from Bethlehem, which means "house of bread." Now isn't it ironic that in the "house of bread" there's a famine? It doesn't matter where you are; the famines of life will find you.

The man is of the tribe of Judah: the royal tribe, the tribe of kings, the tribe of the future Messiah and King. He is married and has two sons. His life is maturing well.

An Uprooting (verse 1d)

> went to live for a while in the land of Moab.

The man moves his family to Moab. The uprooting of a family is not a casual matter. This man is moving his family out of the local community. They move beyond the range of local visits, and there is no record of return trips. This is good-bye to family and friends.

It becomes apparent later in our story that this man is a landowner. He sells his land to finance the move and a new start somewhere else. Technically, he doesn't sell his land but leases it.

A Custom of Land Ownership

Before Israel entered the promised land, the Lord gave instructions to apportion the land by lot to the tribes and clans of Israel.* After Joshua led Israel in the conquest of Canaan, he apportioned

---

* The instructions for apportioning the land were given to Moses in Numbers 26:52–56.

the land to each of the tribes and clans of Israel according to the instructions of Torah.*

The land became a family inheritance. It could not be sold, but it could be leased. In Torah the Lord says,

> The land must not be sold permanently, because the land is Mine and you are but aliens and My tenants. Throughout the country that you hold as a possession, you must provide for the redemption of the land.
> —Leviticus 25:23–24

The Torah teaches that the land of Israel belongs to God. The Israelites merely lease it from Him. They cannot buy or sell it, but they can lease it for up to forty-nine years. Although this custom isn't observed today, it was in the days of Joshua and in the time of our story, a generation or two after Joshua's death.

The Year of Jubilee

Every fiftieth year is a holy observance, called the year of Jubilee. In Torah the Lord says,

> Count off seven Sabbaths of years—seven times seven years—so that the seven Sabbaths of years amount to a period of forty-nine years. Then have the trumpet sounded everywhere on the tenth day of the seventh month; on the Day of Atonement sound the trumpet throughout your land. Consecrate the fiftieth year and proclaim liberty throughout the land to all its inhabitants. It shall be a jubilee for you; each one of you is to return to his family property and each to his own clan. The fiftieth year shall be a jubilee for you; do not sow and do not reap what grows of itself or harvest the untended vines. For it is a jubilee and is to be holy for you; eat only what is taken directly from the fields.

---

* Joshua's apportioning of the land of Canaan is recorded in Joshua 14:1–5.

> In this year of Jubilee everyone is to return to his own property.
>
> If you sell land to one of your countrymen or buy any from him, do not take advantage of each other. You are to buy on the basis of the number of years since the Jubilee. And he is to sell to you on the basis of the number of years left for harvesting crops. When the years are many, you are to increase the price, and when the years are few, you are to decrease the price, because what he is really selling you is the number of crops.
> —Leviticus 25:8–16

In the forty-ninth year, on the Day of Atonement—Yom Kippur—the activities of Jubilee begin. All land returns to the original owner and family.

Short-term

If someone comes upon difficult times, he may sell or lease his property. That is what Elimelech has done.

This action may look like a good move in the short term. The farther to the next Jubilee the more money he receives to finance his move and a new start. However, it puts him and his family at risk in the interim, because they have given up their inheritance.

Long-term

Fortunately the lease is no longer than forty-nine years to the next Year of Jubilee. The land will revert back to his descendants in future generations.

The Move

This move to Moab is questionable. The issue is not the geographical movement from one place to another. It is the moving away from the people of God to a people who do not believe in

Him. Elimelech and his family are leaving the fellowship of believers.

Even in the finest families there are black sheep and children who make bad choices. Why is he leaving the "house of bread" in Israel to go to another country? Has God told him to do so? There is no indication. Is this disbelief in God? Probably. Is there a problem? I suspect so.

A Deeper Problem (verse 2a)

> The man's name was Elimelech, and his wife's name was Naomi. The names of his two sons were Mahlon and Kilion.

Upbringing

Scripture gives us background into the family. The man's name is Elimelech, which means "my God is king." He has a wonderful name.

He is of the royal tribe, Judah, of Bethlehem, with the testimony in his very name that "my God is king." He comes from a fine family of devout Jewish believers. They are following God and honoring Him in the naming of their son.

The wife's name is Naomi, a commonly used name today that means "pleasant" or "lovely." Three thousand years ago it was also used more strongly to mean "pleasing" or "content." Her parents may have waited a long time to have her. She was a blessing from the Lord that gave them "contentment."

Decision

However, Elimelech apparently took her as his own personal contentment. He wanted her to fill a personal need in his life. When we ask other people to bring us happiness and contentment, they often fail—not because they don't want to please us, but because we are asking too much from them.

Expectations drive our happiness in life. If we expect other people to bring us happiness, pleasure and contentment, we will be disappointed. The other parties will also be disappointed, because they do not succeed. In reality, it was an unreasonable expectation in the first place.

His choice is a mistake. We need to be content in ourselves and our God. Other people add to our lives, but cannot fill our basic needs. Elimelech is expecting too much of Naomi.

Consequences

The consequences of Elimelech's mistake appear in the names of his two sons. One was named Mahlon, which means "pining away." The other was named Kilion, which means "dissipation."

Mahlon is probably the older, because he is named first. He is the introvert, pining away alone. Kilion is the extrovert, dissipating his energies. Both names imply that they're headed for self-destruction.

Here's the picture: "my God is king" marries "my contentment," and the results are "pining away" and "dissipation."

There is a problem in the family. The leader has sought personal satisfaction and didn't find it. Because he did not seek God, he does not have the power of God in his life to strengthen and guide him. He feels empty and disappointed. He pines away and dissipates his energies.

A Contradiction (verse 2b)

They were Ephrathites from Bethlehem, Judah.

The scribe seems shocked as he repeats, "They were Ephrathites from Bethlehem, Judah." Ephrathah means "I will make him fruitful."

Ephrathah is a leading clan in Bethlehem. Elimelech is a man of leadership heritage. He should be standing in the famine and encouraging others to do the same. In sharp contrast, he leaves to seek relief in another land.

Without God's strength in his life, the man cannot stand in the famine, let alone strengthen others. The course he has chosen has left him empty. He chooses to leave—a second bad choice.

The Destination (verse 2c)

And they went to the land of Moab and lived there.

He takes his family to the land of Moab and settles there—a third bad choice. Let me give you a little background on Moab.

National Ties

The Moabites descended from Lot, the nephew of Abraham. They were distant relatives to the Israelites. God wanted them to be considerate and friendly to Israel. But they were not.

A National Incident

After the Israelites left Egypt, they wandered for forty years in the wilderness. Then they headed to the east, past the Dead Sea and north to enter Canaan from the eastern side. They defeated the Amorites and the Ammonites. They then headed for the land of Moab and Midian.

Balak, King of Moab, feared he could not defeat the Israelites after these recent victories, so he hired the prophet Balaam to curse them. Balaam prepared offerings and practiced his rituals to curse them. But God gave him blessings for the Israelites instead, so he blessed them. This scenario occurred three times, infuriating Balak.

When he could not curse the Israelites, Balaam gave Balak and the Midianites another plan. He told them how they could seduce the Israelite men.

It was customary for the Moabites to include sexual rituals as part of the worship of their gods. So Moabite and Midianite women seduced Israelite men and led them in their pagan rituals.

When the Israelites participated in these rituals of idol worship, the Lord became angry and brought a plague against Israel for their rebellion and immorality. The plague was stopped when the high priest thrust a spear through a young Israelite man and Midianite woman, who were engaged in this pagan, sexual ritual. In the interim 24,000 Israelites died.*

Judgment

Before Moses died, he was allowed to bring vengeance. He led the Israelite army to attack and defeat the Moabites and Midianites. They killed the kings and Balaam for their seduction plot that caused so many deaths.

In the law of Moses the Lord says,

> No Ammonite or Moabite or any of his descendants may enter the assembly of the Lord, even down to the tenth generation. For they did not come to meet you with bread and water on your way when you came out of Egypt, and they hired Balaam son of Beor from Pethor in Aram Naharaim to pronounce a curse on you.
> —Deuteronomy 23:3–4

The Moabite seduction of Israelites and Israel's vengeance occurred early in the lifetime of Joshua. These events and judgment were common knowledge during the period of our story.

---

* The account of the Moabite and Midianite seduction of Israelites is found in Numbers 25:1–9.

The Moabites were known for their peaceful but deceptive ways and their pagan sexual rituals. Yet "my God is king" heads to Moab! Unless God had directed him to go to this place, it could only mean trouble. And trouble it was.

THE CONSEQUENCES

Once we have made a choice, God lets us reap the natural consequence of our decisions. God may provide grace in the midst of trouble, and even grant restoration if we turn to Him. But there is no indication that Elimelech ever did.

This is the negative side of our story. It is a stern warning against disobedience and misdirected stubbornness.

Death (verse 3a)

> Now Elimelech, Naomi's husband, died,

"My God is king" died in a foreign land. Perhaps he thought of the choices he had made. Perhaps he had asked himself, "What if?" God gives us choices. But we are responsible for our decisions, and we suffer the consequences.

He could have turned to God and found a way out, but there is no indication that he ever did. He simply died in the consequence of his selfishness—with nothing more than he had when he left Bethlehem: his wife and two sons.

Survival (verse 3b–4a)

> and she was left with her two sons. They took for themselves Moabite wives; the name of the one was Orpah and the second was Ruth.

The wife and two sons continue to live in Moab. Perhaps they have nothing to go home to; perhaps they are too embarrassed to go home. In the meantime the sons find Moabite women and marry them. They follow in their father's footsteps.

While out dissipating his energy, Kilion meets a Moabitess named Orpah. She is the first to marry into the family. Her name means "neck," or one who is "looking back." While he is dissipating his energies, she is looking back to see where they've been.

Eventually Mahlon, the introvert, is brought into social activity. He finds a Moabite bride, named Ruth. (The marriage of Ruth to Mahlon is explicitly confirmed later in our story).

Ruth means "friendship." This meaning of friendship is not just verbal company; it is one who looks after the well being of her neighbor. And "pining away" needs a friend to look after him.

Though it is not yet evident, Ruth is making a decision to follow God. This is the only presentation of God that she has seen. She is responding to Him. God will honor this decision as a step in the right direction. But for now, it looks like disaster.

More Death (verse 4b)

> After they had lived there about ten years, the two sons also died, Mahlon and Kilion;

They stayed for ten years, and the two sons died. There is no indication of why or how the sons died. We do know they were young and in the first ten years of their only marriage. Their deaths are premature and tragic. They leave widows without children.

Destitution (verse 5)

> and Naomi was left without her two sons and her husband.

Naomi is now deserted and heartbroken. She has lost her husband and two sons. Her life has become destitute with running, death, survival, and more death. She has seen enough and run out of choices. She is a widow in a foreign land with nothing left and nowhere to turn.

It seems God often waits until we run out of options and become desperate. Only then do we truly rely on Him. We realize that He is the only one who can get us out of our difficult and often hopeless situation.

Chapter 1 Spiritual Pearl:

Not following God results in disappointment, emptiness, disaster, and sometimes premature death.

CHAPTER TWO

THE DECISION TO FOLLOW GOD

INTRODUCTION

Chapter 2 Progress

In chapter 1 the man of the house made bad decisions that cost the lives of the family men. In this chapter each of the remaining women faces a crossroads decision in her life. One stays in Moab. Two return to Bethlehem, to God's people and His ways.

Biblical Text

> [6]When she heard in Moab that the Lord had visited His people by giving them bread, Naomi and her daughters-in-law prepared to return from the land of Moab. [7]With her two daughters-in-law she set out from the place where she had been living, and they went on the road to return to the land of Judah.
>
> [8]Then Naomi said to her two daughters-in-law, "Return, each of you, to your mother's home. May the Lord show kindness to you, as you have shown to your dead and to me. [9]May the Lord grant each of you to find the rest of a wife in the home of another husband."

Then she kissed them, and they wept aloud [10]and said to her, "We will return with you to your people."

[11]But Naomi said, "Return again, my daughters. Why would you come with me? Am I going to have any more sons, and would they become your husbands? [12]Return, my daughters, go. I am too old to have another husband. Even if I thought there was still hope for me—even if I had a husband tonight and then gave birth to sons—[13]then would you wait for them until they grew up? Would you remain unmarried for them? No, my daughters. It is more bitter for me than for you, because the Lord's hand has gone out against me!"

[14]At this they wept again. Then Orpah kissed her mother-in-law good-bye, but Ruth clung to her. [15]"Look," said Naomi, "your sister-in-law is going back to her people and to her gods. Go back with her."

[16]But Ruth replied, "Don't urge me to leave you or to turn back from you. Where you go I will go, and where you stay I will stay. Your people will be my people and your God my God. [17]Where you die I will die, and there I will be buried. May the Lord deal with me, be it ever so severely, if anything but death separates you and me."

Ruth 1:15 "Look," said Naomi, "your sister-in-law is going back to her people and her gods. Go back with her."

[18]When Naomi realized that Ruth was determined to go with her, she stopped urging her.

[19]So the two women went on until they came to Bethlehem. [20]When they arrived in Bethlehem, the whole town was stirred because of them, and the women exclaimed, "Can this be Naomi?"

[21]"Don't call me Naomi," she told them. "Call me Mara, because the Almighty has made my life very bitter. I went away full, but the Lord has brought me back empty. Why call me Naomi? The Lord has afflicted me; the Almighty has brought misfortune upon me."

[22]So Naomi returned from Moab, accompanied by Ruth the Moabitess, her daughter-in-law, arriving in Bethlehem as the barley harvest was beginning.

—Ruth 1:6–22

Ruth 1:22 So Naomi returned from Moab accompanied by Ruth the Moabitess, her daughter-in-law, arriving in Bethlehem as the barley harvest was beginning.

Key Spiritual Principle: A commitment decision is needed to follow God

As humans our decision-making process is heavily influenced by circumstances. In this hectic society our lives are bombarded with a hundred choices that needed to be made yesterday. It is difficult to look beyond the panics in our lives to make sound, long-term decisions.

In the time of Ruth the people of God were geographically centered in Israel. When Elimelech left Judah, he was leaving God's people, the people following God's ways.

Our story focuses not on the tragic deaths in Moab, but on God's kindness that blesses Naomi and her daughter-in-law after they return to Bethlehem. Even out of our wanderings, God can bring good to our lives and glory to His name. But first, we need to make a commitment decision.

This chapter depicts life-long decisions to follow God and associate with His people: first by Naomi, then Orpah and Ruth.

Naomi's Decision

Naomi has survived the terrible consequences of bad decisions for the past decade. Her life was devastated by the tragic deaths of her husband and two sons, her entire family. She endured, demonstrating courage and character.

In the wake of these tragedies God presents an opportunity. She now makes a good decision for herself and what's left of her life.

A Word from the Lord (verse 6a)

> When she heard in Moab that the Lord had visited His people by giving them bread,

Naomi had maintained contact with Israel. God sent word to her that He had ended the famine and provided food to His people in Bethlehem, "house of bread."

God reached Naomi with the hope that He does come through. It's not a rainbow, but it is a ray of hope. Perhaps in the famine of her life God will provide for her, too.

Naomi's Response (verse 6b)

> Naomi and her daughters-in-law prepared to return from the land of Moab.

Naomi decides to return home to the people of God and His ways. Moab was never home for her. Only Judah is home: God's land with God's people and His ways. She prepares to leave Moab.

Naomi's Commitment (verse 7)

> With her two daughters-in-law she set out from the place where she had been living, and they went on the road to return to the land of Judah.

Naomi acts on the good word she has received. She sets out with her two daughters-in-law and heads on the road that leads to Judah. Her actions demonstrate her commitment to follow God.

Naomi is moving toward God. When we take just a few steps in His direction, He takes giant leaps to come to us. The result of Naomi's few steps is the God-provided, happy ending to this story. But much more is yet to happen.

Orpah's Decision

As Naomi sets out on her journey, it occurs to her that her daughters-in-law may not share her desire to return to Bethlehem, to God's ways and His people. Naomi made the right choice, but so must each of the daughters-in-law. Each must choose, of her own accord, the path to follow.

Second Thoughts (verse 8)

> Then Naomi said to her two daughters-in-law, "Return, each of you, to your mother's home."

Naomi is not upset nor angry with her daughters-in-law. She appreciates the kindness they have shown her and is thinking of their well being.

Two Moabite daughters-in-law would have difficulty fitting and being accepted into a Jewish community. They were better known and had greater acceptance in Moab. Naomi is trying to save them the trials of living in a strange land, as she has done for the past ten years. Her words are intended to determine whether they are ready to make this trip.

A Parting Blessing (verse 9a)

> "May the Lord show kindness to you, as you have shown to your dead and to me. May the Lord grant each of you to find the peace of a wife in the home of another husband."

Naomi calls the Lord's blessing on these young women. Obviously they have been good wives and daughters-in-law. She wishes them well.

Naomi considers a young, single woman restless until she finds rest and peace in marriage. Her daughters-in-law are still young, and she wishes them the peace and happiness of a wife in a new marriage.

Their Response (verse 9b)

> Then she kissed them, and they wept aloud

Their response is admirable. It is based on their love and appreciation for Naomi. These women have endured the deaths of their husbands together. Through shared tragedy they have become close-knit. The young women care for Naomi.

An Initial Decision (verse 10)

> and said to her, "We will return with you to your people."

Their emotions are true and strong but not an adequate basis for the tough road ahead. They need to consider the consequences resulting from this decision. They are still in an emotional state and not ready to make a commitment.

Naomi realizes the emotion of their immediate response and tests their decision. She gives them a lesson on the hard facts of life.

Practicality—1 (verse 11)

> But Naomi said, "Return again, my daughters. Why would you come with me? Am I going to have any more sons, and would they become your husbands?"

Naomi encourages them to return, and questions their decision to follow her. They need to think about their opportunities.

They need to know that she cannot provide husbands for them. She doesn't have any other sons for them to marry, nor is she pregnant that she would have another son for them.

Practicality—2 (verse 12)

> Return, my daughters, go. I am too old to have another husband. Even if I thought there was still hope for me—even if I had a husband tonight and then gave birth to sons, then would you wait for them until they grew up?

Again Naomi urges them to return to their own people, where their best opportunity for marriage resides.

Even if Naomi were to find a husband today and have more sons, it would be too long before they would become old enough to marry these daughters-in-law. No matter how much she would like to help them, Naomi cannot help them.

Practicality—3 (verse 13)

> "Would you remain unmarried for them? No, my daughters. It is more bitter for me than for you, because the Lord's hand has gone out against me!"

These women couldn't wait twenty years for a son to be born and grow up. They have been married less than ten years and are widows. They are young and need to remarry.

Naomi blames her problems on the Lord. I don't believe that the Lord has actively worked against her. She has lived the consequences of bad decisions. Those decisions brought the tragic deaths of her husband and sons.

Tragic events may occur in anyone's life. It is common to blame our problems on someone else, especially God. Sometimes we just blame the combination of circumstances. Sometimes we blame ourselves.

Naomi is now headed in the right direction, but her emotions are still bitter with tragedy and loss. She fears that people around her will also experience tragedy. Perhaps if these girls weren't with her, they would not experience further tragedy.

Practicality says, "Stay in Moab."

A Final Decision (verse 14a)

> At this they wept again. Then Orpah kissed her mother-in-law good-bye,

To one, the practicality speech was enough. Orpah kissed her mother-in-law and returned to her people, the place she had known, the place of most likely opportunity. She chooses practicality.

There is nothing wrong with practicality. It should characterize our lives. The problem is the old gods in Moab. There are no believers, no worshippers of the true God, no one following God's ways there.

Practicality is important, but the spiritual aspect needs to be the overriding consideration. It wasn't to Orpah. There was a new path to take, but she wasn't ready for an arduous trip. She had always been "looking back." Now she went back.

Without spiritual hope, she may get a life, but she passes up an opportunity for eternal life.

Ruth's Decision

Now it is Ruth's turn to make a decision. She reveals surprising character and commitment.

A Commitment Decision (verse 14b)

> but Ruth stayed close to her.

To the other, practicality was not enough. Ruth, "friendship," stays close to Naomi. She is a loyal friend.

Ruth is looking for something more. Somehow through this family in trouble, Ruth sees something she admires, something she wants. The Lord has shown Himself to her and is calling her. She responds to Him by staying close to Naomi—her only link to Him.

The stories of people turning to the Lord are unique and sometimes involve someone who is living a less-than-righteous life.

In the New Covenant the Apostle Paul speaks of our having the gift of the Holy Spirit in "earthen vessels." I get the picture of a candle inside a clay vase: not much light showing through. Yet God in His Sovereignty still reveals Himself, and many find Him.

Naomi's Counter (verse 15)

> And she said, "Behold, your sister-in-law has returned to her people and to her gods. Return after your sister-in-law."

Naomi has no idea of the depth of commitment Ruth possesses. Naomi gives her another chance. But Ruth does not want to go back neither to her people nor to those gods. She has chosen the living God.

Naomi's persistence elicits a response of insight and commitment from the inner soul of this young widow.

Ruth's Declaration (verse 16–17)

> But Ruth replied, "Do not urge me to leave you or to turn back from you. Where you go I will go, and where you stay I will stay. Your people will be my people and your God my God. Where you die I will die, and there I will be buried. May the Lord deal with me, be it ever so severely, if anything but death separates you and me."

What a commitment! Ruth clearly and emphatically states her resolution to follow Naomi and the Lord.

"Do not urge me to leave or turn back" demonstrates intent and resolve. Since Naomi had twice requested her to return, Ruth asks Naomi for the courtesy of respecting her decision. Ruth speaks straight from her heart.

This soliloquy is called the seven-fold commitment:

- Where you go I will go—a commitment of actions, traveling together, doing the same things.
- Where you stay I will stay—a commitment of association, being together, residing and living together.
- Your people will be my people—a commitment of identity, leaving her own family and people and joining Naomi's people. Ruth is converting and changing her identity from Moabite to Israelite.
- Your God will be my God—a commitment of spiritual worship and lifestyle. She commits to forsake the gods of Moab and their religious practices and to follow the Lord in a holy lifestyle.
- Where you die I will die—a commitment to death. She has already committed every aspect of her life: what she does, where she lives, who she is and how she worships. She now commits to remain with Naomi until she dies.
- And there will I be buried—the commitment to Ruth's death. Just in case it sounds like her commitment would end in Naomi's death, Ruth promises to maintain this lifestyle until she dies and then be buried with Naomi: association in and past death.
- May He deal with me ever so severely if anything but death separates you and me—she intends to stick like glue to Naomi; only death will separate them.

She closes with an oath to the Lord, her new God in her new lifestyle. She has no intention of doing anything less.

Ruth exhibits character in her resolve and commitment to Naomi and to God. Incredibly, Ruth keeps these promises completely for the rest of her life—without remorse, without wavering, without exception!

Naomi's Acquiescence (verse 18)

> When Naomi realized that Ruth was determined to go with her, she stopped urging her.

"Determined?" That is putting it mildly. I am not sure Naomi was strong enough to stop her. Naomi realizes the commitment in the heart of this young lady. She allows Ruth to accompany her on the journey home to Judah.

THE RESULTS

Naomi's and Ruth's decisions bring them to God's people and the place of His blessing.

Destination Home (verse 19a)

> So the two women went on until they came to Bethlehem.

With resolve like that of these two women, there is no doubt they would reach Judah and Bethlehem, Naomi's hometown. She returns to the "house of bread."

The Women of Bethlehem's Response (verse 19b)

> When they arrived in Bethlehem, the whole town was stirred because of them, and the women exclaimed, "Can this be Naomi?"

What a sight! It's been more than ten years since Naomi left with her husband and two sons. Now she returns with a Moabite daughter-in-law. How incredible! How curious! What does Naomi have to say?

Naomi's Declaration (verse 20)

> "Do not call me Naomi," she told them. "Call me Mara, because the Almighty has made my life very bitter."

She asks not to be called Naomi, "my contentment," but Mara, "bitterness." She's feeling bitterness of soul. Her name is a lie. It doesn't represent her any more. She doesn't even want to hear it. Bitterness better describes her now.

Mara attributes her troubles to the Lord Almighty, "El Shaddai" in Hebrew. She recognizes that he is sovereign. She cannot outrun or avoid Him.

Naomi's Testimony (verse 21)

> "I went away full, but the Lord has brought me back empty. Why call me Naomi? The Lord has afflicted me; the Almighty has brought misfortune upon me."

Truth, yes, but not exactly the kind of testimony we want to hear. It is the honesty of bitterness that comes from experiencing the consequences of bad decisions.

She went away with a husband and two sons: everything she wanted. Without the Lord they disappeared and literally died. She now returns empty. Bitterness has filled her soul. People often respond to difficulties with bitterness and resentment.

Naomi must change her attitude to receive the full benefit of God's blessings. She has turned and made her way back to Bethlehem, to God's people. The Lord will reward her initial step toward Him.

The Lord patiently gives her the next few months of smaller benefits to prepare her for greater blessings. Only He can take a bitter life and make it truly sweet. Only God can turn "bitterness" back into "contentment." And that is what He is going to do.

Return Postscript (verse 22)

> So Naomi returned, and Ruth the Moabitess, her daughter-in-law, was with her, who returned from the land of Moab. They came to Bethlehem as the barley harvest was beginning.

Turnarounds

The returns and turnarounds have begun. First, Naomi is rescued out of Moab and returned to her home and her God. Her husband and two sons were not as fortunate. Second, Ruth, a Moabitess, returns to live with her and worship the living God.

A Date/Time Stamp

There is a date/time stamp: "as the barley harvest was beginning." The barley harvest is the early grain harvest, two to three weeks before the wheat harvest. It typically begins during the Feast of Unleavened Bread and its grain is used for the ceremony of First Fruits. The harvests are generally completed around *Shavuot*, also called the feast of Weeks or Pentecost.

The remainder of our story takes place in the seven-week period between *Pesach*, or Passover, and *Shavuot*, or Pentecost. In our western calendar, this period falls in the spring between late March and early June.

Shavuot

Shavuot is one of seven holy observances in the yearly Jewish calendar. It is also one of three observances a year at which all Jewish men are to present themselves to the Lord. It commemorates the giving of the law and the covenant at Mount Sinai. During the feast of *Shavuot* today Jewish synagogues traditionally read the book of Ruth.

In the New Testament book of Acts, chapter 2, *Shavuot* is called by its Greek name, "Pentecost." It represents the coming of the Holy Spirit and the beginning of a new covenant described in Jeremiah 31.

CHAPTER 2 SPIRITUAL PEARL:

THE DECISION TO FOLLOW GOD MAY BE DIFFICULT, BUT IT IS THE ONLY PATH THAT LEADS TO HOPE AND FULFILLMENT. IT INCLUDES ADHERING TO HIS WAYS AND ASSOCIATING WITH HIS PEOPLE.

CHAPTER THREE

THE ACTIONS OF FOLLOWING GOD

INTRODUCTION

Chapter 3 Progress

Chapter 3 presents Ruth and Naomi adjusting to life in Bethlehem. Ruth goes into the fields and works to provide food for herself and her mother-in-law. She demonstrates consideration, politeness, and a good work ethic.

Boaz enters the story as the landowner. He demonstrates courtesy, kindness, protection, and special consideration to this foreigner who has come to work in his field.

Through circumstances God orchestrates their encounter. They need to remain faithful to God's ways to realize the potential benefit of this relationship.

Biblical Text

> [1]Now Naomi had a relative on her husband's side from the clan of Elimelech, a man of standing and character, whose name was Boaz.

²And Ruth the Moabitess said to Naomi, "Let me go to the fields and pick up the leftover grain behind anyone in whose eyes I find favor."

³Naomi said to her, "Go ahead, my daughter." So she went out and began to glean in the fields behind the harvesters. As it turned out, she found herself working in the field belonging to Boaz, who was from the clan of Elimelech.

⁴Just then Boaz arrived from Bethlehem and greeted the harvesters, "The Lord be with you!"

"The Lord bless you!" they called back.

⁵Boaz asked the foreman of his harvesters, "Whose young woman is that?"

⁶The foreman replied, "She is the Moabitess who returned with Naomi from the land of Moab." ⁷She said, "Please let me glean and gather among the sheaves behind the harvesters." She went into the field and has worked steadily from morning till now, except for a short rest in the shelter.

⁸So Boaz said to Ruth, "My daughter, listen to me. Don't go and glean in another field and don't go away from here. Stay here with my young girls. ⁹Watch the field where the men are harvesting, and follow along after the girls. I have told the young men not to touch you. And whenever you are thirsty, go and get a drink from the water jars the men have filled."

¹⁰At this, she bowed down with her face to the ground. She exclaimed, "Why have I found favor in your eyes that you notice me—a foreigner?"

¹¹Boaz replied, "I've been told all about what you've done for your mother-in-law since the death of your husband—how you left your father and mother and your homeland and came to live with a people you did not know before. ¹²May the Lord repay you for what you have done. May you be richly rewarded by the Lord, the God of Israel, under whose wings you have come to take refuge."

¹³"May I continue to find favor in your eyes, my lord," she said. "You have given me comfort and have spoken kindly to

Ruth 2:16 Rather, pull out some stalks for her from the bundles and leave them for her to pick up, and don't rebuke her.

your servant—though I do not have the standing of one of your servant girls."

[14]At mealtime Boaz said to her, "Come over here. Have some bread and dip it in the wine vinegar." When she sat down with the harvesters, he offered her some roasted grain. She ate until she was satisfied and had some left over.

[15]As she got up to glean, Boaz gave orders to his young men, "Even if she gathers among the sheaves, do not embarrass her. [16]Rather, pull out some stalks for her from the bundles and leave them for her to pick up, and don't rebuke her."

—Ruth 2:1–16

Key Spiritual Principle: Following God includes making ethical choices in the circumstances of daily life

The decision to follow God needs to be demonstrated in the actions of one's life. A one-time decision with no further evidence is dubious. The subsequent actions verify the level of decision commitment.

Some people are born with a consistent character. They make up their minds to do something and never stray. Their actions remain consistent with their decisions.

When we decide to follow God, His Spirit joins our spirit to strengthen our faithfulness in following Him. For consistent people, He strengthens the natural character they possess.

Ruth was one of these naturally consistent people. Her actions demonstrate the commitment of her decision to follow God.

THE GOD OF CIRCUMSTANCE

Roles
God's Role

We call our God the God of history, because we believe he controls the destiny of human history. There is room in this belief for individuals to make their own decisions and do what they want. However, as the course of history unfolds, God's overall will prevails.

We call Him the God of circumstance, because we believe He actively controls or passively influences the circumstances in our lives. The more we pray, the more actively He participates in our lives and circumstances.

Coincidences that bear spiritual benefits are often examples of God's intervention in our lives through serendipitous events. My friend has a sign on his living room wall that reads: "A coincidence is a small miracle where God chose to remain anonymous."

Our Role

We believe that God loves us and adds benefit to our lives as we follow His ways. If we make a mistake and return to God, He rescues us from the full negative impact of our circumstances. If we don't pray or acknowledge God, He may let our lives be overrun by the natural consequences of our actions and other people's activities.

Following God doesn't mean we won't suffer hardships. Hardships are a normal part of life. Naomi and Ruth have already endured personal difficulties and tragedy.

Sometimes we struggle with trusting God. We may be disappointed with our progress or circumstance and try to help God with our life's plan.

There is a danger in not waiting to follow God. We may move too quickly or in the wrong direction and miss benefits God has for us. We are challenged to keep our commitment and trust God to act in our behalf.

Ruth

Then there's Ruth. Without hesitation she faithfully follows Naomi and the customs of God's people. She works through the circumstances in her life, and good things begin to happen.

The Extended Family (verse 1)

> Now Naomi had a relative on her husband's side from the clan of Elimelech, a man of standing and character, whose name was Boaz.

Boaz

Family is important to the Lord. The book of Ruth revolves around one clan and the establishing of a godly family.

Here the scribe introduces the man who will become the hero of our story. He is a man of standing and reputation.

When the famine struck he stayed in Bethlehem, and God blessed him. This man has made a life decision to follow God. His spiritual character is demonstrated as the story unfolds.

Boaz's Name

The name Boaz means "in Him is strength." To Boaz the "Him" refers to the Lord God. The "strength" here is intensified strength or power, which is certainly true of our God.

This word is used generations later by King Solomon in naming the two huge bronze pillars on the porch of the great temple of the Lord in Jerusalem. The pillar on the right he named *Jakin*, or "He judges." The pillar on the left he named, *Boaz*, or "in Him is strength," the same as this name in our story. Both pillars reflect reverence to the Lord God, to Whom the temple was built.

A Little Family Background
Another National Incident

A generation or two earlier, Joshua had led the Israelites in the conquest of Canaan. Their first battle was at the high-walled city of Jericho. Joshua sent spies to scout the city. They were helped by a prostitute named Rahab. She told the spies,

> "I know that the Lord has given this land to you and that a great fear of you has fallen on us. . . . our hearts melted and everyone's

courage failed because of you, for the Lord your God is God in heaven above and on the earth below. Now then, please swear to me by the Lord that you will show kindness to my family, because I have shown kindness to you. Give me a sure sign that you will spare the lives of my father and mother, my brothers and sisters, and all who belong to them, and that you will save us from death."

—Joshua 2:10–13

A Convert

Rahab believed in the God of Israel. She risked her life and jeopardized her family, when she hid the spies and misdirected the men of Jericho's army. In the New Covenant book of Hebrews, Rahab is recognized as a woman of faith for her actions.

She helped the spies escape, and they promised to spare her and her family. In Joshua 6, when Israel conquered Jericho, Joshua sent these spies to Rahab's house to rescue her and her family. They lived among the Israelites throughout the lifetime of Joshua.

The Family Link

The account in Joshua isn't clear on Rahab's marital status. The family with her was father, mother, brothers, and sisters. There is no mention of a husband or children of her own.

The New Testament genealogy of Matthew 1 indicates that Rahab later married an Israelite named Salmon, of the tribe of Judah. They had at least one son, Boaz: the same Boaz who is introduced here and plays a key role in our story.

Priorities

Because of Rahab's past experience and foreign heritage, there was probably much scrutiny of her life and actions. She obviously learned to be faithful and discreet in this small community, because nothing negative is ever mentioned about her.

Rahab was faithful to the Lord and His ways. The fact that her son became a man of standing and reputation testifies to the character of this household.

Coming from this environment, Boaz would be careful in his actions yet considerate to foreigners. And so he is. His name, "in Him is strength," also has a related idea: "in Him is safety" or "protection." Boaz will provide both to Ruth, first protection, later strength.

A Harvest Custom
The Practice
God had given a harvest custom that provides food for the less fortunate. As a follower of Torah, Boaz observed this custom. The law was given by Moses.

> When you are harvesting in your field and you overlook a sheaf, do not go back to get it. Leave it for the alien, the fatherless and the widow, so that the Lord your God may bless you in all the work of your hands.
> —Deuteronomy 24:14

The harvesters were to pass through the crop only once to pick the grain. They were not to return a second time. This harvesting would leave grain that was not quite ripe or overlooked. (The passage applies a comparable instruction to harvesting olives from trees or grapes from vines. They were to harvest only once, and leave the remaining crop for the needy.)

The Beneficiaries
The alien, fatherless, and widows were allowed to pick the leftover crop behind the harvesters. This picking of leftover crops was called "gleaning." It may not have been the best of the crop, but it was healthy food. Also they worked for it, just like the harvesters.

Ruth clearly fit the qualifications:
- an alien—she is an outsider, from Moab.
- fatherless—she had left her family, and her father-in-law was dead.
- a widow—her husband was dead.

She was all three.

Ruth's Suggestion (verse 2)

> And Ruth the Moabitess said to Naomi, "Let me go to the fields and pick up the leftover grain behind anyone in whose eyes I find favor."

Naomi does not have to talk to Ruth about working. Ruth picks up on this custom and suggests to Naomi that she go into the fields to glean. She is anxious to do whatever she can to provide for herself and her mother-in-law.

It's a relief to have Ruth offer to help. Apparently there is little left of the money from the sale/lease of their property. They need to make do as best they can.

Ruth realizes that gleaning may not be easy. The fields may be crowded, and some may not want another stranger there. She needs someone to give her the opportunity to work. She may need someone's favor to glean enough to feed her and her mother-in-law.

Naomi's Approval (verse 3a)

> Naomi said to her, "Go ahead, my daughter."

Ruth is a widow herself, yet she stays obedient to her mother-in-law. She offers to work but waits for her mother-in-law's approval.

She is devoted to Naomi and to the Lord. Naomi gives her approval and perhaps some advice.

Gleaning (verse 3b)

> So she went out and began to glean in the fields behind the harvesters.

Regardless of the obstacles, Ruth has the courage to make good her offer. She goes out in the fields to glean, and good things start to happen.

Happenstance (verse 3c)

> As it turned out, she found herself working in the field belonging to Boaz, who was from the clan of Elimelech.

She did not know about distant-cousin Boaz. Ruth just went where she saw a good field and started to work. The Lord led her to the field of cousin Boaz. As in Ruth's case, God usually works through the circumstances of our lives.

Enter Boaz (verse 4)

> Just then Boaz arrived from Bethlehem and greeted the harvesters, "The Lord be with you!"
> "The Lord bless you!" they called back.

What about Boaz? His first words are a reminder that true blessings come from the Lord. Here is a man that follows Torah in his words and actions.

The workers respond in kind, "The Lord bless you." Obviously they have learned that as the Lord blesses Boaz, he passes the blessings on to them. Their response is one of appreciation to God and to their boss.

He Notices Ruth (verse 5)

> Boaz asked the foreman of his harvesters, "Whose young woman is that?"

Now, apparently Ruth possessed as much beauty as friendliness. As soon as Boaz has greeted his workers, he doesn't ask about the harvest or the progress. He asks about the new woman in the field.

The Foreman's Report

The foreman is responsible for people and progress in the field. He knew who she was and reported the account to his boss, the owner of the field. Perhaps he had found out when she asked him for permission to glean in the field.

Who She Is (verse 6)

> The foreman replied, "She is the Moabitess who returned with Naomi from the land of Moab."

In a small community there are no secrets. Everyone has heard about the return of Naomi with a Moabite daughter-in-law. The foreman reports that she is the Moabitess people have been talking about. Perhaps Boaz suspected as much from her appearance.

What She Said (verse 7a)

> "She said, 'Please let me glean and gather among the sheaves behind the harvesters.'"

This young lady has manners. She asked the foreman, using the word "please." Her character is reflected in her manners and work ethic.

What She Has Done (verse 7b)

> "She went into the field and has worked steadily from morning till now, except for a short rest in the shelter."

The foreman reports on her actions. She arrived in the morning for a full day's work and worked hard all day, except for a rest break. She is not lazy. She works hard and long.
Boaz directly goes to talk with Ruth.

Her Surprise
Meanwhile Ruth is in the fields with the rest of the workers. There's talk about Boaz, the owner of the field. He greets his workers, talks a minute to his foreman and heads directly toward Ruth.

She is probably overhearing the gossip and watching. Her interest turns to shock as he heads directly toward her. What can it be? She has obtained permission to glean; she has followed the rules. Why is he coming to her? She is probably nervous as the owner of the field approaches.

HUMAN RESPONSE

Although our God is the God of history and circumstance, He still requires us to be responsible for our actions. He provides the opportunities, but we need to respond to Him in faith and obedience. His opportunities are not for us to squander, but to use for His kingdom. We need to follow His ways faithfully.

It takes obedience to realize and enjoy the full benefit of His blessings. We see both Ruth and her relative Boaz acting obediently, discreetly, above reproach in their first encounter and throughout their courtship.

Boaz's Welcome (verse 8)

> So Boaz said to Ruth, "My daughter, listen to me. Do not go and glean in another field and do not go away from here. Stay close to my young girls."

What a relief! There is nothing wrong. Boaz has come to welcome her and show her kindness.

He comes to her in the practicality of her situation and demonstrates sensitivity and consideration. He addresses her with respect and kindness, as a daughter. Not that she is his daughter, but as part of the community. He invites her to stay and glean behind his girls working the fields. He is giving her an opportunity to work.

Boaz's Instruction (verse 9a)

> Watch the field where the men are harvesting, and follow along after the young girls.

He has both men and women working; apparently the men go first then the women follow. He tells Ruth to follow after the women. He is helping her with the customs so she can follow protocol.

He has a personal understanding of this problem. His mother was a foreigner. He probably remembers difficulties she and the family had adjusting to life among the Israelites.

Boaz's Protection (verse 9b)

> I have told the young men not to touch you.

It is difficult for a woman in a strange land to be out on her own working all day. Her speech betrays her identity, and she barely knows the customs. She is clearly an outsider and could be mistreated. Who would care?

Boaz reassures her that he has told his men not to touch her. She will be safe here under the protection of Boaz, "in him is protection."

Boaz's Special Offer (verse 9c)

> And whenever you are thirsty, go and get a drink from the water jars the young men have filled."

The men are important. He needs to take care of them so that they can harvest the crop. He provides water and food for them as they work.

He makes a special offer to Ruth. She may drink from the water supply he has provided to his workers. It is hot working the harvest in the fields. He offers her water, so that she will remain physically well and not be overcome by the sun.

He is showing sensitivity to her situation and needs:
- to her need for food, offering her an opportunity to work
- to her foreignness, instructing her in the customs
- to her safety, telling the men to leave her alone
- to her well-being, providing water in the scorching sun

Boaz gives her attention and consideration, and she responds in kind.

Her Response—Respect and Gratitude (verse 10)

> At this, she bowed down with her face to the ground. She exclaimed, "Why have I found favor in your eyes that you notice me—a foreigner?"

She may have been nervous, but she recovers quickly. She responds with immediate humility and gratitude. Her bowing to the ground is not slavery or groveling. It is appreciation and respect for this man of standing, who has come to show her kindness.

She is not afraid. She probes with a leading question, "Why have you noticed *me*?" She realizes that this is more than usual treatment. She wants to know why he's being so kind. Does he expect anything from her in response to his overtures?

His Response—Respect (verse 11)

> Boaz replied, "I have certainly been told all about what you have done for your mother-in-law since the death of your husband—how you left your father and mother and your homeland and came to live with a people you did not know before."

Amazing isn't it? The word that is out on Ruth is all good and true. Boaz has heard the whole story, and he's impressed.

Notice his response. She asked why he took notice of her. He responds that it is because of what she has done for her mother-in-law. Her actions, devotion and commitment have impressed him.

He is stating the reason for his interest—her character—which becomes the basis of their relationship. This relationship is not based on looks or physical attraction, though they may be present. It is based on character.

His Response—Blessing (verse 12)

> "May the Lord repay you for what you have done. May you be richly rewarded by the Lord, the God of Israel, under whose wings you have come to take refuge."

In the middle of his field with this foreign woman, Boaz gives her a blessing in the name of the Lord. These are the actions of a man who lives his faith.

When we take refuge in God, He takes care of and rewards us. Boaz entreats the Lord's blessing on Ruth. Little does he know that this blessing to her will return as a blessing to him.

There is also a male response to protect a female who has come under his auspices. Since Ruth has come into his field, he feels responsible to give her oversight and protection, as his name implies. He is a man of moral character who will treat her with respect and courtesy.

Her Response—Opening Up (verse 13)

> "May I continue to find favor in your eyes, my lord," she said. "You have given me comfort and have spoken to the heart of your lowly servant—though I do not have the standing of one of your lowly servant girls."

"May I *continue* to find favor in your eyes"—a favor based on the report he mentioned. She intends to maintain her reputation of commitment and faithful actions. If he is interested in character, then she too is interested in a relationship.

Only now does she open up to him. She admits that he has touched her heart with his consideration and kindness. She is concerned about having enough food, following the customs, her personal safety and health. He has allayed some of her concerns and given her reassurance.

She returns to courtesy and humility. She is working with the young women in the field but places herself below them and below the servants doing menial work. Perhaps she's reminding this man of means that she is just a poor widow working in his fields. I don't think he cares, as he makes the next move.

Their First Date (verse 14)

> At mealtime Boaz said to her, "Come over here. Have some bread and dip it in the wine vinegar." When she sat down with the harvesters, he offered her some roasted grain. She ate until she was satisfied and had some left over.

He returns to invite her to lunch. His workers have beaten out barley kernels and roasted them. They eat freshly roasted grain beside the field. This is a healthy, simple meal that he provides to his workers and eats himself.

He includes Ruth in this luncheon courtesy. Ruth's home-packed lunch, if any, was minimal. This food is extra fuel to keep up her strength and health through the day's work.

This encounter is discreet. She is with him in a group of his harvesters, both male and female. There is nothing about what they said, but he offers her more food than she needs. It is a time of rest and talking in the midst of a hard day's work. (I might add, getting to know someone at work is a good way to learn what the person is really like.)

She then packs some leftover grain and returns to the field.

His Move—Graciousness (verse 15)

> As she got up to glean, Boaz gave orders to his young men, "Even if she gathers among the sheaves, do not embarrass her."

Behind the scenes Boaz increases her special treatment. The rules were clear: you glean behind the harvesters and take only what they leave. Boaz tells his men to make an exception in her case: if she gets ahead of the harvesters, it's okay. Do not embarrass her; just let it go.

His Move—Generosity (verse 16)

> "Rather, pull out some stalks for her from the bundles and leave them for her to pick up, and do not rebuke her."

But what if she doesn't break the rules? She wouldn't break them intentionally. He goes out of his way to help her. He tells his young men that as they are putting bundles together, to set aside some stalks and leave them for her.

He wants to make sure that no one discourages her. He encourages her to return by giving to her what he has to offer—grain from his field.

CHAPTER 3 SPIRITUAL PEARL:

FOLLOWING GOD REQUIRES CHARACTER,
MAKING THE RIGHT MORAL CHOICES
IN THE CIRCUMSTANCES OF LIFE.

CHAPTER FOUR
───────────

THE BENEFIT OF FOLLOWING GOD

INTRODUCTION

Chapter 4 Progress

In chapter 3 Ruth goes into the fields to work so that she and Naomi have food. The field owner encourages and protects Ruth.

In chapter 4 we see the benefits of Ruth's hard work. She brings home more food than she and her mother-in-law need. Her mother-in-law sees the benefit and blesses the man who helped her. She also mentions customs that provide opportunity for additional benefits to them both.

Biblical Text

> [17]So Ruth gleaned in the field until evening. Then she threshed the barley she had gathered, and it amounted to about 3/5 of a bushel. [18]She carried it back to town, and her mother-in-law saw how much she had gathered. Ruth also brought out and gave her what she had left over after she had eaten enough.

¹⁹Her mother-in-law asked her, "Where did you glean today? Where did you work? Blessed be the man who took notice of you!"

Ruth told her mother-in-law about the one at whose place she had been working. "The name of the man I worked with today is Boaz," she said.

²⁰"The Lord bless him!" Naomi said to her daughter-in-law. "He has not stopped showing his kindness to the living and the dead." She added, "That man is our close relative; he is one of our kinsman-redeemers."

²¹Then Ruth the Moabitess said, "He even said to me, 'Stay with my workers until they have finished harvesting all my grain.'"

²²Naomi said to Ruth her daughter-in-law, "It will be good for you, my daughter, to go with his girls, because in someone else's field you might be harmed."

²³So she stayed close to the servant girls of Boaz to glean until the barley and wheat harvests were finished. And she lived with her mother-in-law.

—Ruth 2:17–23

Key Spiritual Principle: God rewards those who follow His ways

Does following God's way always pay off? Sometimes it doesn't seem like it.

There are those who say we should follow God because it's the right thing to do, regardless of the benefits. They are right. God's way is a better way of life, which in itself is a benefit.

However, God does reward those who follow Him. The New Covenant author of the book of Hebrews devotes a chapter to recounting stories of great men and women of faith from the Old Testament, including Abel, Enoch, Noah, Abraham, Sarah, Isaac, Jacob, Joseph, Moses, and Rahab (Boaz's mother). At the beginning of this chapter the author says,

And without faith it is impossible to please God. For he who comes to God must believe that He exists and that He rewards those who diligently seek Him.
—Hebrews 11:6

These great men and women of faith believed God would reward them for obedience to His ways. This belief contributed to their great faith.

As humans we need to know that God will reward us for being faithful and obedient. As Creator of the universe, He is certainly capable of rewarding us. He has also promised to reward us.

In the Old Testament we read,

Lions may grow weak and hungry, but those who seek the Lord lack no good thing.
—Psalm 34:10

The blessing of the Lord brings wealth, and He adds no trouble to it.
—Proverbs 10:22

Proverbs 10:22 The blessing of the Lord brings wealth, and he adds no trouble to it.

> Delight yourself in the Lord, and He will give you the desires of your heart.
> —Psalm 37:4

His reward is seldom material things or the obvious wants. Sometimes it takes a while in coming. Sometimes we need to be in tune with reality to understand how gracious the Lord has been. The result of following God's way is always beneficial. Sometimes it includes money, but it is always more than money can buy.

The Resulting Benefit

God's ways aren't glamorous, but they have benefits: honest work, legal wages, trustworthy friends and spiritual substance. As Ruth follows God's ways, she continues to work and reap the benefit for herself and her mother-in-law.

Barley From Boaz (verse 17)

> So Ruth gleaned in the field until evening. Then she threshed the barley she had gathered, and it amounted to about 3/5 of a bushel.

It isn't manna from heaven; it is barley from Boaz. The work is not over. Once she picks or gleans the grain she threshes or beats out the barley kernels. The result is more than four gallons of dry weight volume. This is a big bundle that does not just fit in one's pocket. Ruth obviously has something to carry her gleanings in.

Returning Home (verse 18a)

> She set out and came to town,

She carries the barley back to town to her mother-in-law. She stays at home and remains faithful to Naomi.

A Benefit Shared (verse 18b)

> and her mother-in-law saw how much she had gathered. Ruth also brought out and gave her what she had left over after she was satisfied.

She is open and honest in her dealings. She went for herself and her mother-in-law, and she returns to show her mother-in-law the benefit she has received.

Ruth brings out the roasted barley left over from lunch. She had saved a little to show her mother-in-law how well she was treated. Naomi picks up on the picture quickly.

A Mother-in-law's Perception (verse 19a)

> Her mother-in-law asked her, "Where did you glean today? Where did you work? Blessed be the man who took notice of you!"

Naomi realizes that this measure of barley is more than normal. Perhaps this was not the first day she went out gleaning. Perhaps Naomi had seen others and knew what to expect. Either way, she knew this was well above average.

She even suspected that the benefit came from a man. Perhaps only men owned the fields. Perhaps she knew Ruth was going to a man's field. Perhaps she suspected a man's intervention from the look on Ruth's face. Perhaps it was just an older woman's intuition. However it happened, Naomi perceived that a man had noticed Ruth.

Naomi blesses the man. She is grateful to him for rewarding them generously. She knows that the more God blesses this man, the more he is able to bless them.

Though Naomi has little, she is not greedy. She is willing to work for what they get and is grateful and considerate to those who help them. She has character and sets an example for Ruth.

The Day's Report (verse 19b)

> Then Ruth told her mother-in-law about the one at whose place she had been working, and she said, "The name of the man I worked with today is Boaz."

Naomi is excited as Ruth relates the story, detail by detail. It is interesting that to Boaz she called herself "less than a lowly servant," but to Naomi she is working "with" Boaz. She didn't feel like a servant. He didn't treat her like a servant. But the man's name is "Boaz."

A Mother-in-law's Blessing (verse 20a)

> Naomi said to her daughter-in-law, "The Lord bless him! He has not stopped showing his kindness to the living and the dead."

Naomi recognizes the name Boaz, and blesses him for his generosity to them. The reference to "the living" is for Naomi and Ruth. The reference to "the dead" is for her deceased husband and two sons. He is respecting the dead by showing kindness to the widows.

That "he has not stopped" indicates that he was generous in the past. He continues to demonstrate good reputation, character, consideration and generosity.

A Greater Benefit

God's purposes are always far-reaching. They provide help in the present and greater benefit in the future. While we are wrestling with the issues and emotions of today, He is watching over our good for eternity.

Our God is a God of design. As we continue to follow Him obediently, His plans unfold and blessings materialize.

There is more at issue here than a man and a woman meeting in a field. There is a greater plan of character and seed for the lineage of King David and our Messiah. Of course, these issues do not appear until later, and only because these two are faithful and obedient in the present.

We need to remember that whatever we are doing has consequences beyond the present, extending to the future for eternal purposes. We are not faithful for what is seen, but for what is unseen. As the New Covenant author says, "We walk by faith and not by sight."

Yet, sometimes we catch a glimmer of what's in store.

A Custom of Land Redemption (verse 20b)

> Naomi added, "This man is our close relative; he is one of our kinsman-redeemers."

Naomi adds a comment of glimmering hope. The land would revert to her or her husband's descendants in the Year of Jubilee, but that's probably too far away to help her. However, a close relative could redeem the land for her sooner. In Torah the Lord says,

> If one of your countrymen becomes poor and sells some of his property, *his nearest relative is to come and redeem* what his countryman has sold. If however, he has no one to redeem it, . . . if

he does not acquire the means to repay him (the buyer), what he sold will remain in the possession of the buyer until the Year of Jubilee. It will be returned in the Jubilee, and he can then go back to his property. [Italics added for emphasis]
—Leviticus 25:25–28

If an alien or a temporary resident among you becomes rich and one of your countrymen becomes poor and sells himself to the alien living among you or to a member of the alien's clan, he retains the right of redemption after he has sold himself. One of his relatives may redeem him: an uncle or a cousin or *any blood relative* in his clan may redeem him. Or if he prospers, he may redeem himself. [Italics added for emphasis]
—Leviticus 25:47–49

If a brother needs to sell or lease his land, a close relative, called a redeemer, or *Goel* in Hebrew, may buy back the land for him. The *Goel* relationship may be extended to include any blood relative. Logically the closest relative is a brother.

A Custom of Childless Widow Redemption

The redeemer concept also applies to a childless widow. In Torah the next brother is to marry his childless sister-in-law.

If brothers are living together and one of them dies without a son, his widow must not marry outside the family. Her husband's brother shall take her and marry her and fulfill the duty of a brother-in-law to her. The first son she bears shall carry on the name of the dead brother, so that his name will not be blotted out from Israel.
—Deuteronomy 25:5–6

The brother, or next closest relative, becomes the husband of a childless widow and allows the firstborn to carry on the deceased husband's name. The son receives the inheritance of the deceased husband. Thus the closest blood relative becomes redeemer for both the childless widow and the land.

The kinsman-redeemer is part of God's social welfare program. Families are to take care of each other. The immediate family is the basic unit of care, next the extended family and relatives.

In this instance Boaz is not only of the same tribe, but also of the same clan, making him an eligible kinsman-redeemer. If Boaz is the closest relative, he can redeem Naomi's land by buying the land of her husband's inheritance, and redeem Ruth by marrying her and raising a son in her deceased husband's name. The son would receive Elimelech's inheritance from Naomi.

Naomi has adopted the name of Mara, or "bitterness," because of the difficulties and tragedy in her life. For the first time there is hope of a light toward the end of this tunnel. Our God gives hope to the hopeless, and only He can bring this hope to reality.

The Day's Report—Continued (verse 21)

> Then Ruth the Moabitess said, "He even said to me, 'Stay close to my young workers until they complete all my harvest.'"

Ruth continues to recount her meeting with Boaz. She remembers his offer to continue working in his fields. After the success of the day's work, she is encouraged to return to his fields, especially by his courteous and special treatment.

Naomi's Advice (verse 22)

> Naomi said to Ruth her daughter-in-law, "It will be good for you, my daughter, to go with his young girls, that harm not fall upon you in the field of another."

The possibility of harm is always there, but they need the food. Why risk it, when there is a courteous man offering protection and special consideration? It is the obvious decision, confirmed by his behavior and reputation.

I cannot help but wonder if Naomi is thinking beyond the field to the customs of the kinsman-redeemer. There might be something more in the offing than this season's grain and food. She might be harboring a glimmer of hope for restoration that only God can provide.

Ruth's Obedience (verse 23a)

> So she stayed close to the young girls of Boaz to glean until the barley and wheat harvests were finished.

Ruth follows the instructions of her mother-in-law and Boaz. She returns to work the fields of Boaz under the protection of his young girls and his instructions to the young men. She works through the barley harvest, then the wheat harvest.

She is not taken out of the situation. She is rescued in it. God has provided her work with special treatment that will take care of her and her mother-in-law.

She continues to work through what is before her. Part of her situation is a relationship with Boaz that is growing and will eventually require resolution.

Ruth's Behavior (verse 23b)

> And she lived with her mother-in-law.

Here is an interesting epilogue. There may have been opportunity to get more personal with Boaz. But no. The record is clear. She stayed with her mother-in-law. She was discreet, above reproach.

She has asked for nothing. She has taken nothing for granted. She has worked hard. She has behaved properly. She exudes character.

I am sure that Boaz is impressed not only by her outward appearance, but also by her faithfulness, diligence and character. She is the kind of woman described in Proverbs 31—a godly woman.

> **CHAPTER 4 SPIRITUAL PEARL:**
>
> GOD REWARDS FAITHFUL CHARACTER AND OBEDIENCE.

CHAPTER FIVE

THE CHALLENGE OF FOLLOWING GOD

INTRODUCTION

Chapter 5 Progress

In this chapter Naomi formulates a plan to determine whether Boaz is interested in helping them as a kinsman-redeemer. Ruth executes the plan perfectly.

There's a flaw in the plan—a closer kinsman-redeemer. Boaz offers to resolve the issue and provide them with a solution. The problem is that the solution may not be him.

Biblical Text

> [1]One day Naomi her mother-in-law said to her, "My daughter, should I not try to find a home for you, where you will be provided for? [2]Is not Boaz, with whose servant girls you have been, a kinsman of ours? Tonight he will be winnowing barley on the threshing floor."
>
> [3]"Wash and perfume yourself, and put on your best clothes. Then go down to the threshing floor, but don't let him know

you are there until he has finished eating and drinking. ⁴When he lies down, note the place where he is lying. Then go and uncover his feet and lie down. He will tell you what to do."

⁵"I will do whatever you say," Ruth answered. ⁶So she went down to the threshing floor and did everything her mother-in-law told her to do.

⁷When Boaz had finished eating and drinking and was in good spirits, he went over to lie down at the far end of the grain pile. Ruth approached quietly, uncovered his feet and lay down. ⁸In the middle of the night something startled the man, and he turned and discovered a woman lying at his feet.

⁹"Who are you?" he asked.

"I am your servant Ruth," she said. "Spread the corner of your garment over me, since you are a kinsman-redeemer."

¹⁰"The Lord bless you, my daughter," he replied. "This kindness is greater than that which you showed earlier: You have not run after the younger men, whether rich or poor. ¹¹And now, my daughter, don't be afraid. I will do for you all you ask. All my fellow townsmen know that you are a woman of noble character."

¹²"Although it is true that I am near of kin, there is a kinsman-redeemer nearer than I. ¹³Stay here for the night, in the morning if he wants to redeem, good; let him redeem. But if he is not willing, as surely as the Lord lives, I will do it. Lie here until morning."

—Ruth 3:1–13

Key Spiritual Principle: Perseverance is required in trusting God

In this chapter the relationship of Ruth and Boaz progresses from interest to engagement: the peak of romance. This is the story of a gentleman and a lady developing a relationship with respect and responsibility. There is emotion, amusement, conversation, interaction, appreciation, and a word not in fashion today—commitment.

Ruth 3:3 Wash and perfume yourself, and put on your best clothes. Then go down to the threshing floor, but don't let him know you are there until he has finished eating and drinking.

There is also a road block that cannot be avoided. It needs to be addressed and resolved, following spiritual, ethical values and customs.

Sometimes we get the impression that life should be easy when we are following God. Not true. The closer I get to God the more difficulties and obstacles obstruct my path. These circumstances need to be resolved by trusting God and adhering to His ways.

Boaz and Ruth have the courage to face life's obstacles and the faith to follow God's ways in resolving them.

A Marriage Plan

The man has shown interest and consideration. It is time for Ruth to reciprocate. Naomi, the wise mother-in-law, formulates a plan. Ruth, the faithful daughter-in-law, follows it to the letter.

Naomi's Consideration (verse 1)

> Naomi her mother-in-law said to her, "My daughter, should I not seek the solace of a wife for you, that would be good for you?"

Naomi has grown to appreciate and love her daughter-in-law. She now calls her "my daughter." Ruth is the only daughter she has known. They have become close-knit through shared tragedy and more than a decade of surviving together.

In chapter 2 Naomi blessed both daughters-in-law and suggested they return to find the place of solace, or rest, as a wife in the home of another husband. Orpah left, but Ruth remained with Naomi.

Naomi remembers the satisfaction of having her own home with a husband and two sons. It's too late for her to recover the experience.

Naomi wants Ruth to experience marital fulfillment. She is still a young woman, who needs her own husband and home.

Naomi unfolds a plan.

The Prospect (verse 2a)

"And now is not Boaz a kinsman of ours, with whose young girls you have been?"

Naomi has obviously explained to Ruth the role of the kinsman-redeemer. He is qualified to marry the childless widow, Ruth, and redeem the land of Naomi's deceased husband.

They have talked about Boaz, his character, courtesy and wealth. He is qualified to be their kinsman-redeemer. He has shown Ruth special consideration throughout the harvest season.

Naomi senses that Ruth has an appreciation and interest in this man. They have spent two months talking and getting to know one another. He has shown interest in Ruth. It's now time to confirm his intentions.

The Location (verse 2b)

"He will be winnowing barley on the threshing floor tonight."

Naomi knows the routine. It's the end of the harvest, and Boaz will be winnowing his barley at the threshing floor.

In those days they lifted and scattered the grain in the air to let the evening breeze or a fan blow the chaff away from the kernel. The kernels fell to the ground, were sifted and packaged for storage or sale. The chaff and stubble were blown away from the kernels; they were then gathered and burned.

He is preparing to sell his crop and acquire his earnings for the season. The harvest is complete, and the end is in sight. He has probably sold much of his crop already; he simply needs to package and deliver it.

He is about to realize the benefit of the crop he has watched over for several months. He has done this many times before, and it is rewarding work. He will be in good spirits.

Naomi has thought through this plan. Now is the time to approach him. It is time for action.

Preparation (verse 3a)

"Bathe, perfume, change and dress yourself up and then wander down to the threshing floor."

What young lady has not heard these words, "It is time to look your best"? This is not over-dressed; this is dressed well. These are two widows living on minimum wage. They do not have much, but they do have a little perfume and a good dress.

Ruth has the natural friendliness that has already caught Boaz's interest. He has seen her in working clothes for days on end. It's now time to surprise him with the dressed-up version.

This "wandering down to the threshing floor" is a casual stroll to destiny. This woman only appears casual. She is on a mission. Her steps are certain. She will end up in Boaz's presence.

Instructions

Naomi gives Ruth explicit instructions for her part in this plan.

Wait (verse 3b)

"But do not let him know you are there until he has finished eating and drinking."

She is not to interrupt, but to wait. Let him finish his celebration over the harvest and settle down to rest. He will be relaxed, as he prepares for the night's sleep.

Observe (verse 4a)

"When he lies down, note the place where he is lying."

She is to note where he lies down, so that she can find him later in the dark, when everyone else has gone to sleep. She needs to know where he is to follow the next instruction.

Uncover (verse 4b)

"Then go and uncover his feet and lie down. He will tell you what to do."

This is discreetly public: not so public as a scene, yet not so private as alone. There are others around, who would sense any disturbance or commotion. This is a quiet, personal encounter.

These would be unusual instructions in today's culture. This symbolic action is linked to a custom. She is to lift up the edge of his blanket and lie down at his feet. This action is not meant to be erotic. She is symbolically asking him to be her covering, to provide for and take care of her. This is the role of a husband, and she is asking him to fulfill this role to her.

It is a moving scene. She is not arrogant, nor begging. She is making a physical action with significance that requires a response. She is making a proposal that leads to marriage. He must now respond.

The man has little choice. His only other option is to pass on Ruth, and she is too good to pass up. It is all over but the celebrating!

Ruth's Response (verse 5)

And she said to her, "I will do all that you have said."

Ruth is an impressive woman. She agrees to follow all her mother-in-law's instructions. When Ruth makes a commitment, she keeps it, as was demonstrated in chapter 2. She will follow these instructions accurately, completely, without wavering.

These women have been through a great deal together: the deaths of their husbands, the journey back to Bethlehem and finding a way to survive together. They are an unbeatable team: Naomi, the wise planner, and Ruth, a woman committed to executing Naomi's instructions.

THE EXECUTION

The execution of this plan takes courage and character. Ruth has plenty of both. Naomi waits expectantly for the outcome.

Ruth's Actions (verse 6)

> So she wandered down to the threshing floor and did everything her mother-in-law instructed her to do.

There is usually a difference between a plan and reality. Often quick thinking and minor changes are required. Ruth follows the plan as instructed to realize the desired outcome.

The Scene (verse 7a)

> When Boaz had finished eating and drinking and was in good spirits, he went over to lie down at the far end of the grain pile.

Is Naomi calling this one right? It's just as she predicted. He has been celebrating. He is in good spirits and has gone to the far end of the grain pile to lie down for the night.

In Position (verse 7b)

She approached quietly, uncovered his feet and lay down.

Ruth follows directions right on queue. She approaches quietly, lifts up the corner of his blanket and lies down at his feet. The situation is set. All she has to do now is wait.

A Propitious Event (verse 8)

In the middle of the night the man was startled, and he turned and discovered a woman lying at his feet.

In the middle of the night something startles him. Perhaps it is from God; perhaps from Ruth. No matter. He awakes to discover this woman lying at his feet. She was quietly waiting for him and the encounter of her life.

The Encounter (verse 9)

"Who are you?" he asked.

"I am your humble servant Ruth," she said. "Spread the corner of your garment over your servant, since you are a kinsman-redeemer."

All he did was ask who she was. She identifies herself and proposes marriage!

She identifies herself as his humble servant, not of lower status but as an equal with humility. She asks him to spread the corner of his garment over her, symbolically covering her as a husband.

Though symbolic, her request is direct. She points out that this request is appropriate, because he is a kinsman-redeemer. He is an appropriate relative to become her husband.

He may have been asleep when he asked the question, but he's wide-awake now! Boaz recognizes her voice. He understands this unusual proposal and responds affirmatively.

Boaz's Response (verse 10)

> "The Lord bless you, my daughter" he replied. "This kindness is greater than that which you showed earlier, because you have not gone after the choice young men, whether rich or poor."

Reaction

He is delighted and honored that this woman of character has come to him. He enjoyed their afternoon lunches and considered them a kindness. He considers this proposal a much greater kindness. She could have gone for a younger man, but she did not. He is thrilled.

Thoughts on Age

Apparently she is much younger than he is. Naomi stayed in Moab ten years, and Ruth was married and widowed. If she married in her late teens or early twenties, she may now be in her late twenties or early thirties.

Boaz is obviously older, maybe forty to fifty years of age. Moses, Joshua, and Caleb stayed virile to 100 to 120 years of age; so Boaz still has time to have children.

Older and Alone

There is no indication that Boaz has ever been married. Why not? He has had plenty of time to find someone. Yet he has found no one.

He has been looking for a woman of character, but it's been difficult for him to find someone appropriate. Perhaps the local reputable families still hold his mother's foreign heritage or past against him.

Rahab's background makes it even more important that his actions be circumspect, above reproach. Here he is: middle aged, of reputation and alone.

He has waited long for a woman of character to take interest in him. He is surprised when Ruth does. Perhaps he is just humble. I suspect he's been disappointed more than once at the deferral of marriage hopes.

Hope

How long does one maintain hope? How long does one continue expectantly? How long does it take before one just accepts life the way it is and makes what one can of it? He has made what he can of his life: property and reputation.

> Hope deferred makes the heart sick; but when desire comes, it is a tree of life.
> —Proverbs 13:12

He is interested in the young lady, but needed her response before going any further. There's no point in making a fool of himself uselessly.

Opportunity

He felt she had other opportunities because of her age, friendliness and reputation. However, she has come to him. His responds immediately, delighted with her decision.

He will move quickly to bring this relationship to fruition. He has waited twenty years or more for this opportunity: a compatible woman of character interested in him. He will not let her get away without exercising every possible, appropriate action.

Boaz's Answer (verse 11)

> "And now, my daughter, do not be afraid, because I will do for you all that you ask. For the leaders of my people know that you are a woman of noble character."

Commitment

Boaz now reassures her of his positive response. She need not be afraid. He will do all she has asked. He will marry her and redeem her mother-in-law's land.

He understands the full ramifications of this responsibility and promises to fulfill it. He is not shrinking from responsibility. He acknowledges, understands and accepts it completely.

Obviously he has thought about this possibility prior to her arrival. He has looked into the extent of this responsibility and is now ready to commit to her.

He is in love. He responds to protect and provide for her and her mother-in-law, as an expression of his love and devotion.

Noble Character

Notice how important her noble character is to him. He mentions it here to highlight the reason for his love. Why is he interested in this foreign beauty? Is it her looks? Her hard work? More: it's her noble character.

Now, here is a challenge: go into a foreign country, as an outsider, a widow and the daughter-in-law of a widow, and become recognized by the people of that new country as a person of noble character. This is what Ruth has accomplished in one harvest season, only a couple of months long.

A Fly in the Ointment (verse 12)

> "It is true that I am a kinsman-redeemer, there is a kinsman-redeemer closer than I."

His words hit her like a hammer. Her body tenses and turns cold. Her hopes plummet—like an anchor into a dark, ocean abyss.

Boaz may not be the one! He is kind, considerate, of noble character and good standing. The possibilities from here go only downhill.

What will become of her? She fights through the shock and disappointment to hear everything Boaz is telling her.

Boaz proposes a plan amendment. He has examined this possibility. The custom places the first obligation on the nearest blood relative. Only if the closer relative refuses to perform the duties of a kinsman-redeemer can Boaz step in and become her husband.

The Fine Print in the Redemption Custom

We read earlier that a man is to marry his brother's childless widow and name the first son after his brother. Torah also addresses the man who will not perform this duty:

> However, if a man does not want to marry his brother's wife, she shall go to the elders of the town gate and say, "My husband's brother refuses to carry on his brother's name in Israel. He will not fulfill the duty of a brother-in-law to me."
>
> Then the elders of his town shall summon him and talk to him. If he persists in saying, "I do not want to marry her," his brother's widow shall go up to him in the presence of the elders, take off one of his sandals, spit in his face and say, "This is what is done to the man who will not build up his brother's family line."

That man's line shall be known in Israel as "the family of the unsandaled."
—Deuteronomy 25:7–10

What a custom! There is clearly pressure on the brother or closest relative to perform the duty of a redeemer to his sister-in-law. He has the right of refusal, but he will be brought before the city elders, spit in the face and given the name of "unsandaled," a stigma on one's family in that society.

A Plan Adjustment

Boaz has thought through the custom and its fine print. He too has a plan. The problem is that his plan cannot guarantee that he and Ruth will be together. He can ensure that Ruth will be taken care of by a kinsman-redeemer, but it may not be him.

Boaz's Instructions (verse 13a)

"Stay here for the night, . . ."

Boaz's instructions start with Ruth and her well being. All his dialogue in this book begins with consideration for Ruth. Here he simply asks her remain where she is until morning. This is not an opportunity for indiscretion. It is simply safer to remain there than to go out in the late night.

The Down Side (verse 13b)

"in the morning if he wants to redeem you, good; let him redeem;"

There is no other way. If the other man wants to redeem Ruth and Naomi, then Boaz has to step back and let him. At least Ruth and Naomi will be cared for.

It is not his favorite solution, but a solution nonetheless. It is the only way to get through this negative option to the option he hopes to find.

"No" responses are tough. They offend our egos, especially the male ego. However, often we need to endure "No" responses to get to the best "Yes" response.

Boaz is required to check out the option of the closer kinsman-redeemer. He's hoping for a "No" response from the closer kinsman-redeemer, so that he can obtain a "Yes" response to take Ruth as his wife.

The Promise (verse 13c)

> "But if he is not willing to redeem you, then I myself will redeem you, as surely as the Lord lives."

These are the words she came to hear this night: a promise from the man she loves that he will take care of her. He understands her desire and makes his commitment to her. Boaz promises in the name of his Lord, the God of Israel, that he will fulfill this obligation. He has promised everything that she hoped he would. Further, he has promised to resolve this roadblock and to take care of her, one way or the other. It is not the outcome she had hoped for, but the man she has trusted will do all he can. That is as much as she can ask.

In the "fine print" it is the place of the sister-in-law to confront the brother before the town elders. Boaz assumes this responsibility, saving Ruth the embarrassment.

A Final Instruction (verse 13d)

> "Lie here until morning."

For now there is nothing more to do. He has discussed the alternatives. There is only one responsible course of action.

Tonight she can just lie here safely at his feet until morning, covered by the corner of his robes. This is not a demeaning or servile place. It is a safe place under his protection.

Perhaps it is the last time they will be together. Perhaps it is the first of many to come. Only the Lord knows for sure.

Chapter 5 Spiritual Pearl:

God's path often presents difficulties that need to be resolved by following God's ways and trusting Him for the best outcome.

CHAPTER SIX

THE PRACTICE OF WAITING WITH GOD

INTRODUCTION

Chapter 6 Progress

In this chapter Ruth waits until morning and returns to her mother-in-law with a gift of grain from Boaz. She reports on the results of their plan execution.

She then waits with her mother-in-law and prays for God and the man she loves to bring legal and personal matters to the best conclusion.

Biblical Text

> [14]So she lay at his feet until morning, but got up before anyone could be recognized; and he said, "Don't let it be known that a woman came to the threshing floor."
>
> [15]He also said, "Bring me the shawl you are wearing and hold it out." When she did so, he poured into it six measures of barley and put it on her. Then she went back to town.

¹⁶When Ruth came to her mother-in-law, Naomi asked, "How did it go, my daughter?" Then she told her everything Boaz had done for her ¹⁷and added, "He gave me these six measures of barley, saying, 'Don't go back to your mother-in-law empty-handed.'"

¹⁸Then Naomi said, "Wait, my daughter, until you find out what happens. For the man will not rest until the matter is settled today."

—Ruth 3:14–18

Key Spiritual Principle: Waiting is a good time for prayer

Who says that following God is easy? It's not. Both Ruth and Boaz have roles to perform to bring their relationship to fruition. Ruth has to wait—perhaps the harder role.

Waiting is a common practice among believers. It is required to act in accordance with God's will and timing. The timing is as important as the action, if we are to receive the desired results.

In our modern society we are pressured to work quickly. There is a fast rate of change, especially in our technologies. However, even here timing is important. We have a saying, "Timing is everything!"

Often the right timing requires waiting. Waiting is a good time for prayer.

RUTH'S ROLE

Ruth's actions and responses indicate that she is interested in marriage and family. When we first meet Ruth she is married and then widowed.

Then she left her land, family and gods to commit to Naomi, a foreign people and their God for her life. When Ruth first came, Naomi presented the prospect of marriage as distant. Yet Ruth joined her on the journey to a new place, a new people and God.

The barley fields are not the voguish place to meet people. They are where the needy work for daily food. This work is not disgraceful; it is honest work. It is God's way to provide food for the less fortunate.

Ruth is in a foreign country, with unfamiliar customs, among strangers, following the ways of this new God. She has placed her devotion to Naomi and her God first, and personal satisfaction second. God is now going to reward her for her commitment and priorities.

Ruth is in Israel only one season, and the Lord provides a man of wealth and character to be her husband. She did not seek him. She found him by chance. In fact he found and approached her. He is everything she wanted: male, considerate, reputable, wealthy and available.

She remains circumspect at all times. She follows her mother-in-law's instructions to let this man know that she is interested and that the customs have provided for their relationship.

Now there is a delay. She must trust this man to bring their mutual dreams to reality. She must trust the Lord God, Who brought them together, to materialize this relationship.

Ruth has found a God Who is faithful and a man who is true. She is about to be blessed by both.

What we do know about these plans is that each member will execute his or her role completely, properly, and without wavering. They are people of commitment.

Morning (verse 14a)

> So she lay at his feet until morning, but got up before a man could recognize his friends,

I like this expression, "before a man could recognize his friends." This is dark. Although behaving appropriately, they did not want cause a disturbance. So they took precaution.

Protection (verse 14b)

> and he said, "Do not let it be known that a woman came to the threshing floor."

If there is someone else to be involved, they do not want to embarrass anyone or give any false impressions. They are being careful.

Consideration (verse 15a)

> He also said, "Bring me the shawl which is upon you and hold it out." When she held it out, he poured into it six measures of barley and set it on her.

Boaz pours six measures of threshed barley into her shawl and helps Ruth set the load for her journey back to town. The barley is a gift to Naomi to demonstrate his consideration for both of them.
Perhaps he realizes that Ruth came not just on her own, that someone was behind the scenes guiding her. He is thanking that person behind the scenes. He is grateful to all involved.

Return (verse 15b)

> Then she went back to town.

The only thing left for Ruth to do is to return to town. She reports these events to her mother-in-law and waits.

Ruth's Waiting

Ruth has the tough job of waiting. We often need to wait. Generally we simply need to pray for direction. We may get direction to wait longer.

God has a bird's-eye view of what's going on. He knows best when to wait and when to proceed. It is now time to wait.

People often say, "I'm waiting on God." This expression can leave the impression that we are ready but God isn't. Not true. He is always ready. He is generally waiting on us.

Waiting is tough, because we are impatient. However, it is often needed to get all of the circumstances and events in place. It's also needed to get us ready to receive the responsibility or benefit that will be bestowed on us.

We need to be waiting with the Lord, trusting Him for the right outcome. We also need to pray about the events that are occurring. Waiting and praying help us to be in sync with Him and ready to respond appropriately to whatever happens.

In this instance waiting is extra difficult because the coming events will change Ruth's life. She doesn't know what will happen. She's not even participating in the decision-making process. She has no further voice or influence. She feels helpless. She can only wait.

She is trusting Boaz to do what is best and right. She also has faith in the Lord. He has led her this far; He will not let her down. Now she waits, and does some serious praying.

Status Report (verse 16)

> When Ruth came to her mother-in-law, Naomi asked, "How are you, my daughter?" Then she told her everything the man had done for her,

How is she? She is in shock. She followed the plan and did everything she could. But there's a roadblock in the path.

Naomi knew nothing of the closer kinsman or additional plans required. She is surprised to hear what has happened.

Ruth focuses on what Boaz had done for her. She knows that Boaz is committed to her and will do whatever is required to bring them together.

Consideration (verse 17)

> and she said, "He gave me these six measures of barley, saying, 'Do not go back empty-handed to your mother-in-law.'"

Ruth reports that Boaz sent the barley for Naomi. He recognizes that you marry the whole family, not just one person. He makes an overture to Naomi for her consideration and support.

Advice (verse 18)

> Then Naomi said, "Wait, my daughter, until you know how the matter will fall, for the man will not be dissuaded until the matter is settled today."

The wise mother-in-law confirms that Ruth's role is to wait for the results. She also knows the desire of a man to marry the woman he loves as quickly as possible. He will be focused and single-minded. She expects him to resolve this matter that very day.

Legalities

What a desirable society: to be able to resolve a legal matter in one day! We have places where one can get married in one day, but not where issues of responsibility and formal customs can be resolved as quickly. The law calls for swift execution of justice, but long bureaucratic processes encumber it.

There needs to be a balance between legalities and realities. The legalities are needed to formalize and confirm commitments, for example, adopting a child already living with you. Yet, if they take long periods of time, people give up on the legality, because reality supersedes it. We need a balance.

Boaz has both the desire and the means to resolve this legal matter in one day. He is going to the local court. The case will be heard and adjudicated in less than an hour. There will be a legal, formal, public conclusion to this matter.

This approach does have a drawback: the decision is final. He must present his case properly and carefully. He gets only one chance for the outcome he wants. If the court's decision goes against him, he has no recourse.

Chapter 6 Spiritual Pearl:

Following God often requires waiting with God in prayer.

CHAPTER SEVEN

THE TRIAL OF FOLLOWING GOD

INTRODUCTION

Chapter 7 Progress

In this chapter Boaz goes to the town gate—to court. He presents the legal case for redemption of Naomi's property and marriage to Ruth.

Someone else has the first right of redemption. He must present the case fairly and clearly to the court. The court will render a final decision. He is hoping and praying that this decision will bring him a desirable and long-awaited wife.

Biblical Text

> [1]Meanwhile Boaz went up to the town gate and sat there. When the kinsman-redeemer he had mentioned came along, Boaz said, "Come over here, my friend, and sit down." So he went over and sat down.
> [2]Boaz took ten of the elders of the town and said, "Sit here," and they did so. [3]Then he said to the kinsman-redeemer, "Naomi,

who has come back from Moab, is selling the piece of land that belonged to our brother Elimelech. ⁴I thought I should bring the matter to your attention and suggest that you buy it in the presence of these seated here and in the presence of the elders of my people. If you will redeem it, do so. But if you will not, tell me, so I will know. For no one has the right to redeem it except you, and I am next in line."

"I will redeem it," he said.

⁵Then Boaz said, "On the day you buy the land from Naomi and from Ruth the Moabitess, you acquire the dead man's widow, in order to maintain the name of the dead with his property."

⁶At this, the kinsman-redeemer said, "Then I cannot redeem it, because I might endanger my own inheritance. You redeem it yourself. I cannot do it."

⁷(Now in earlier times in Israel, for the redemption and transfer of property to become final, one party took off his sandal and gave it to the other. This was the method of legalizing transactions in Israel.)

⁸So the kinsman-redeemer said to Boaz, "Buy it yourself." And he removed his sandal.

⁹Then Boaz announced to the elders and all the people, "Today you are witnesses that I have bought from Naomi all the property of Elimelech, Kilion and Mahlon. ¹⁰I have also acquired Ruth the Moabitess, Mahlon's widow, as my wife, in order to maintain the name of the dead with his property, so that his name will not disappear from among his family or from the town records. Today you are witnesses!"

¹¹Then the elders and all those at the gate said, "We are witnesses. May the Lord make the woman who is coming into your home like Rachel and Leah, who together built up the house of Israel. May you have standing in Ephrathah and be famous in Bethlehem. ¹²Through the offspring the Lord gives you by this young woman, may your family be like that of Perez, whom Tamar bore to Judah."

—Ruth 4:1–12

Key Spiritual Principle: We need to resolve conflicts spiritually and ethically

Why is it that, as circumstances close in on us and emotions intensify, we revert to our own ways without trusting the Lord? Did He not give us everything that is worthwhile? The Psalms state,

> No good thing will He withhold from them that walk uprightly.
> —Psalm 84:11

The corollary then, is that the Lord is the source of every good thing. Let me put this statement in a logical form with permutations:

- If it is good, it is from the Lord.
- If it is not good, it is not from the Lord.
- If it is not from the Lord, it is not good. Even the things that come from us, if not from God, will turn out to be detrimental.
- Only those things that come from the Lord are good.

How do we know that what has arrived has come from the Lord? We pray about each situation. Sometimes we sense the leading of God in our lives. Generally we follow opportunities that are in accordance with scriptural teaching, sound ethics, and spiritual values. We then trust God for the outcome that is good and best for us.

Boaz's Role

Boaz acts on behalf of Ruth and himself. He will confront the closer kinsman-redeemer—not an easy job. This task is necessary to realize a relationship with Ruth in accordance with God's laws.

He knows the town and the relative. He has a good reputation here. His presence will be respected. Also he loves this woman and will do everything in his power to resolve the matter quickly and favorably.

He must act in accordance with the custom so that there is no doubt in anyone's mind that his and her actions are appropriate and proper. He acts on behalf of their reputation and in faith that the Lord, Who has brought them together, will reward them for their faithfulness.

There's no indication that Boaz had a specific word from God. Yet, as a godly man, he has surely discussed her in his prayers with God.

This woman of faith and character interests him. She has offered herself to him. He will pursue this path, because of her reputation, their actions and his interest in her. He is convinced that this opportunity is from the Lord.

Boaz has come to the place where he wants only what is from the Lord. On the brink of this great decision, he trusts God to make this beautiful woman his. If the Lord does not, then it was not as good as he thought. If He does, then it is good beyond his dreams.

He now pursues the decision following the custom and trusting the Lord.

The Town Gate (verse 1a)

Then Boaz went up to the town gate and waited there.

Even while Ruth was walking home and talking to Naomi, Boaz had started doing his part. His actions take place at the town gate. The gate from which Elimelech left to forsake his inheritance is the same place to which Boaz returns to redeem it. In life we often return to the same place. Hopefully we have matured some in the interim.

In those days the town gate was more than just a place of entrance and exit to the city. It was the place where legal matters were settled. The elders of the city were the leaders and ruling body. They sat at the town gate to hear and make rulings on criminal and civil matters.

Boaz is going to court, to the elders of the city, to get a formal ruling on this matter. The down side is that the ruling of the elders cannot be revoked. They are the final authority in this town. So he is going for a final decision.

Perhaps he has some reason to believe it will turn out in his favor. But there is no certainty until the case is heard and the elders pass judgment.

The Other Kinsman-redeemer (verse 1b)

> When the kinsman-redeemer he had mentioned came along, Boaz said, "Come over here, my friend, and sit down." So he went over and sat down.

Boaz knows the man and calls him friend; in fact he is a relative. The relative knows that something legal is about to happen, because this is the place where legal matters are settled.

Boaz has asked him to sit here and participate. Boaz has probably placed him in a position before the elders that indicates he has a part in this legal matter. There is no need for him to be reluctant. Boaz has a good reputation and will be fair and open whatever the matter. So the closer kinsman responds to his relative.

Court in Session (verse 2)

> Boaz took ten of the elders of the town and said, "Sit here," and they did so.

The reason they are at the gate is to resolve legal issues, so this activity is common. Apparently ten elders form a legal quorum. They understand what Boaz is doing and are ready to hear his case.

The Case (verse 3–4a)

> Then he said to the kinsman-redeemer, "The piece of land that belonged to our brother Elimelech is being reclaimed by Naomi, who has returned from the land of Moab. I will inform you saying, Buy it in the sight of these seated here and in the sight of the elders of my people. If you will redeem it, redeem it, but if you will not redeem it, tell me, so I will know. For there is no one to redeem it except you, and I am next in line."

Boaz is required by Torah to present the case clearly in front of the elders and court. He starts with the land Naomi is reclaiming as a matter for legal consideration and the purpose of this court hearing.

He reminds them of the land that belonged to their brother, Elimelech. They are not literal brothers of Elimelech, but they are relatives, next of kin. Naomi, Elimelech's widow who returned from Moab, is reclaiming this land. In this context she is asking a relative to redeem it for her, so that she can repossess her inheritance. Boaz presents himself as willing to redeem the land for Naomi.

His strategy addresses the land first. He is giving the relative the opportunity to do a good deed for Naomi, a monetary deed that requires some effort. Perhaps he knows the relative can afford to perform this part of the redemption.

Boaz offers to redeem it—if the kinsman does not—to indicate his willingness. The relative is encouraged to redeem it after Boaz's example. He is also freed from guilt, because if he does not redeem it, Boaz will redeem it. Either way, Naomi will recover her husband's inheritance.

A Business Deal

The land redemption is a business transaction with duration and terms.

Duration

If we remember the law of leasing the land earlier, the land is leased on the basis of the number of crops for up to forty-nine years.

Elimelech left during a famine. He was unable to raise crops on the land, so he leased it. Naomi was in Moab more than ten years. If we estimate from the time of the sale/lease to now, it may have been twelve years or more.

So the buyer, or lessee, has held the land for twelve or so years, raised crops and received income from it. The price of redemption would be up to forty-nine years less the twelve years of crops the owner has received. The redeemer would pay for up to thirty-seven years of crops left to the next Year of Jubilee. At that time the land would revert back to any remaining descendants of Elimelech and Naomi.

We don't know the exact length of lease or buy-back, because we don't know when the last Year of Jubilee occurred. We do believe that the next Year of Jubilee is many years away, or this entire transaction would be meaningless.

Terms

This is probably a reasonable business deal. The redeemer manages the land. He hires the workers to plant, tend and harvest crops on the land. He pays the workers, keeps some of the profits for himself and gives the rest to Naomi, the owner.

We don't know the agreement between a manager and an owner, but it would be financially beneficial for both. The manager makes less money than he does from his own property, but he should realize a profit from the additional land.

Naomi is currently receiving nothing from the land. Under this arrangement she will receive income to support herself for the rest of her life.

The Relative's Response (verse 4b)

And he said, "I will redeem it."

The relative follows Boaz's example and offers to redeem the land for Naomi. The nearer kinsman-redeemer has the good will, capital and time to buy and run this additional property for Naomi.

He accepts this proposition as a reasonable business transaction and does a good deed. He will be well thought of for this act. However, the land is only half the story.

The Rest of the Case (verse 5)

Then Boaz said, "On the day you acquire the land from Naomi, then also you acquire Ruth the Moabitess, the deceased's widow, in order to raise up the name of the deceased with his inheritance."

Boaz has let the relative be generous and perform a good deed for Naomi. It is now time to present the whole story to him to see if he can fulfill all the requirements of the kinsman-redeemer.

He now adds that the kinsman-redeemer not only acquires the land for Naomi but also takes Ruth as his wife and raises the first child to the deceased's name. The whole story is now on the table.

The relative knows the full extent of the commitment. It is his choice. Boaz waits for the decision that will determine his destiny with Ruth.

The Final Response (verse 6)

At this the kinsman-redeemer said, "Then I cannot redeem it for myself, because I might ruin my own inheritance. You redeem it for yourself. You have my right of redemption, because I am not able to redeem it."

No explicit reason is given for why the relative cannot redeem Ruth. Perhaps he is married. Perhaps his family would not accept an outsider. There is indication that it would negatively affect his own estate.

He has already shown good will when he agreed to redeem the land, so it is not that he does not care or is not willing to follow the custom. He simply is not able to fulfill both obligations.

A Final Decision

What a relief! Boaz is ready to shout for joy. The closer relative has backed out. Ruth is to be his wife. What joy! What excitement! This is the answer he had hoped for and maybe even expected.

But you never know, until the final decision is made. In fact, that is what is on Boaz's mind—a final decision. He has the verbal decision he wants. He now proceeds to formalize this decision. That is why he has called this court to session.

A Legal Custom (verse 7)

> (Now in earlier times in Israel, for the redemption and transfer of property to settle any matter, one took off his sandal and gave it to his neighbor. This was a legal testament in Israel.)

The taking off of the sandal was used not only for the redemption abrogation (for the brother who would not marry his brother's childless widow), but is now used for the official transfer of property.

The sandal is probably one step beyond giving a handshake. Giving one's sandal represents a formal, legal transaction.

The Legal Transaction (verse 8)

> So the kinsman-redeemer said to Boaz, "Acquire it yourself." And he removed his sandal.

Boaz now has full authority and legal attestation to redeem Ruth as his wife and Naomi's land. The sandal is removed in front of the court and elders. The relative has declined to perform the role of the kinsman-redeemer and has given permission for Boaz to perform it for himself. The matter is legally settled.

With sandal in hand in front of the court and elders, he now has full legal sanction to marry Ruth. He declares his intentions.

Boaz's Pronouncement (verse 9)

> Then Boaz announced to the elders and all the people, "You are witnesses this day that I have acquired all that belonged to Elimelech and all that belonged to Kilion and Mahlon from Naomi."

Boaz leaves no doubt in anyone's mind of his intentions to fulfill every aspect of the kinsman-redeemer role. He mentions the entire family: Elimelech, Kilion, Mahlon, and Naomi.

It is no wonder he is a man of standing, reputation and character. He demonstrates his knowledge of the law and devotion to it. His actions are respectable and honorable. The elders and court agree.

Boaz's Intentions (verse 10)

> "I have also acquired Ruth the Moabitess, Mahlon's widow, for myself as my wife, in order to raise up the name of the deceased with his inheritance, so that his name will not be cut off from among his family or from the town records. Today you are witnesses!"

He has obviously talked to Ruth and learned that she was married to the older brother, Mahlon. He also adds the detail about raising a son to the deceased's name. His son will acquire the land inheritance of Mahlon.

Since Kilion is dead, the son will also inherit land through his grandmother, Naomi. She will inherit all the land of her husband Elimelech and pass it on to her heir—the child of Ruth and Boaz.

Ruth is to become his wife and bear him children. He is not about to lose this opportunity. It's too important. He has waited too long. He will gladly accept this woman as the one he has waited for to be his wife.

He is a mature, responsible man, ecstatic that his marriage dreams are finally being fulfilled. He is grateful to the God of circumstance, Who brought a woman from another country to convert, demonstrate character, and offer herself to him.

He makes his vows in front of the elders and court at the town gate.

Witnesses (verse 11a)

Then those at the gate and the elders said, "We are witnesses."

The elders and those at the gate affirm that they are witnesses of what has transpired. It appears that everyone wants to get involved in this event. This is an obviously good match—Boaz and Ruth.

The Verdict

The witnesses also recognize that to Boaz the land is secondary. They are aware that Ruth is the focal point of his interest. To the verdict they add blessings to her, him, and their future offspring.

A Blessing to Ruth (verse 11b)

"May the Lord make the woman who is coming into your home like Rachel and Leah, who together built up the house of Israel."

Beyond the call of justice, they give a major blessing to Ruth. Her friendliness and character have won the favor of the local townsfolk.

They suggest that this one woman be like Rachel and Leah, whose sons started the twelve tribes of Israel; their handmaids bore four of the twelve sons. What a blessing! How many sons do they expect this woman to have?

A Blessing to Boaz (verse 11c)

"May you be noble in Ephrathah and be famous in Bethlehem."

They wish for Boaz to become greater. He is noble in Bethlehem. They wish for him to be noble throughout the area of Ephrathah and to become famous in Bethlehem. They are impressed with his knowledge and commitment to Torah. They wish him greater success.

A Blessing to their Offspring (verse 12)

"Through the offspring the Lord gives you by this young woman, may your house be like the house of Perez, whom Tamar bore to Judah."

They further suggest that the offspring be like Perez, whom Tamar bore to Judah. Interesting comparison. Tamar was the daughter-in-law of Judah; she was married to his first son, and then widowed.

The next son refused to perform the duties of a kinsman-redeemer. He lay with her but would not have children by her. God took his life for his disgraceful behavior. Judah sent her away to save the life of his youngest son.

Meanwhile she dressed like a prostitute and waited for Judah, her father-in-law, by the side of the road. As he was on his way to shear his sheep, he stopped, went in and lay with her (not knowing she was Tamar). She became pregnant.

When later he learned it was Tamar, he was embarrassed at his treatment of her. He took her into his home to care for her and the twin sons she bore by him.[*]

Perez is one of the twins sons Tamar bore to Judah. He is the ancestor of those present in Bethlehem. Their blessing is for Ruth to bear a son like their esteemed forefather.

The Townsfolk

There is great rejoicing in Bethlehem, because all in attendance are impressed with the actions of Boaz and the reputation of Ruth. They are convinced this is a good and godly match. Their marriage will enhance and benefit the tribe of Judah, the clan of Ephrathah, and the town of Bethlehem.

It is amazing that when God's will appears, the results become a blessing to everyone involved, near and far. The people of Bethlehem are on the periphery of this blessing. Yet they, too, are blessed, because God's blessings overflow to the entire community.

He is a great God with even greater plans in store for Boaz, Ruth, and Bethlehem, starting with their marriage.

---

[*] The account of Judah and Tamar is found in Genesis 38.

Chapter 7 Spiritual Pearl:

When we follow God through stress and trials, He gives us what is best for us.

Chapter Eight

The Blessings of Following God

Introduction

Chapter 8 Conclusion

In chapter 8 Boaz marries Ruth and redeems Naomi's land. Ruth bears a son for Boaz, and Naomi is blessed with a grandson.

The scribe identifies the greater family tree into which our story fits. They are of the royal tribe of Judah. Their great grandson is Israel's greatest monarch—King David.

Biblical Text

[13] So Boaz took Ruth and she became his wife. Then he went to her, and the Lord enabled her to conceive, and she gave birth to a son.

[14] The women said to Naomi, "Praise be to the Lord, who this day has not left you without a kinsman-redeemer. May he become famous in Israel! [15] He will renew your life and sustain you in your old age. For your daughter-in-law, who loves you and who is better to you than seven sons, has given him birth."

¹⁶Then Naomi took the child, laid him in her lap and cared for him.

¹⁷The women living there said, "Naomi has a son." And they named him Obed. He was the father of Jesse, the father of David.

¹⁸These then are the descendants of Perez:
Perez was the father of Hezron,
¹⁹Hezron the father of Ram,
Ram the father of Aminadab,
²⁰Aminadab the father of Nahshon,
Nahshon the father of Salmon,
²¹Salmon the father of Boaz,
Boaz the father of Obed
²²Obed the father of Jesse, and
Jesse the father of David.

—Ruth 4:13–22

Key Spiritual Principle: God's blessings extend beyond us to our children and grandchildren.

So Boaz marries Ruth. Was there ever any doubt? This is an exciting story with beauty, delays, honor, and blessing. In the end Boaz finds his Ruth, and Naomi acquires her land and a grandson.

There is also a strategic significance to this marriage. Boaz and Ruth become the great grandparents of King David, who established Israel's greatest dynasty. The Davidic dynasty ruled Judah then Israel for more than four centuries from 1015–586 BC.

The Redemption

Boaz redeems both Ruth and Naomi. When he presented the case in court, he talked about the land of Naomi first, then the marriage to Ruth. Now the story focuses on Ruth first, then Naomi.

For Boaz (verse 13)

> So Boaz took Ruth and she became his wife. Then he went to her, and the Lord enabled her to conceive, and she gave birth to a son.

For Boaz the long wait is over. He has found a woman of character and beauty to grace his home: one he can take pride in and appreciate, who will appreciate him. He has a son, who will carry on his relative's name, but the later references always refer to the child as his. Apparently the inheritance is more closely associated with the property than the person.

For Ruth

For Ruth the primary importance is her marriage to Boaz, a man of reputation, consideration and means. He loves her and will take care of her and their only son.

In the back of her mind is her marriage years before, which produced no children. Can she bear children? In this society children are the confirmation of a woman's womanhood. She had no children before, when she was younger. Can she now?

The Lord is a God of grace. He blesses His people in every important way. The text specifically points out that the Lord enabled Ruth to have a son. This biblical expression is generally used when women waited many years to conceive. Again, patience and faithfulness yielded the blessing.

She has now fulfilled her obligation to her husband to bear an heir, and takes on the responsibility of raising the child. This child will be well cared for by his mother and grandmother.

For Naomi

The blessing to Boaz and Ruth is significant and obvious: fulfillment of hope long deferred but realized by the grace of God and their obedience. They have done their part and received their blessing.

The fulfillment to Naomi might be overlooked, except by the text. It elaborates on Naomi. Naomi is blessed with a kinsman-redeemer, an heir, a daughter-in-law, and a grandson.

A Kinsman-redeemer (verse 14a)

> The women said to Naomi, "Blessed be to the Lord who has not left you without a kinsman-redeemer this day."

Boaz brings a major blessing to Naomi with his willingness and performance of the kinsman-redeemer role. There is no way that Naomi by herself could take back her land or have a family.

She was doomed to the life of a lonely, widow, with only the memory of her deceased husband and two sons. Naomi's contentment had been replaced by bitterness. She had no hope, only the desire to finish her life with the people of God.

But God had plans for Naomi. He brought a kinsman-redeemer to redeem her land for her, to marry her daughter-in-law and to give her a grandson.

An Heir (verse 14b–15a)

> "May he become famous in Israel!"
> "He will renew your life and sustain you in your old age."

Another blessing to Naomi is her grandson. His father is a man of stature in the community, but the women wish this child reputation throughout Israel.

A grandchild is a blessing from the Lord that naturally renews the life of the grandparents. This child will renew and sustain Naomi's spirits. He will also take care of her in her old age and manage her land.

A Daughter-in-law (verse 15b)

> "For your daughter-in-law, who loves you and who is better to you than seven sons, has given him birth."

The women note that these blessings all originated from Ruth. They say she is a daughter-in-law who is better than seven sons. What a compliment! How these Jewish women could consider a foreign woman better than seven sons is beyond me.

As an outsider Ruth has won the respect of the entire community for her godly character and her devotion to her mother-in-law. She is the one who bore this child: a blessing and renewal to Naomi in her old age.

A Grandson (verse 16–17a)

> Then Naomi took the child, laid him in her lap and cared for him.
> The women living there said, "Naomi has a son."

Two godly women raise this child. They have long awaited and will dote over him. He will hear the blessings of the Lord from his father, mother, and grandmother, for he is the child of unusual blessing. His heritage and birth are a testimony to the whole community.

Naomi remembers two other sons, who died in a foreign land. That was a difficult and tragic story. This is an experience in renewal, blessing, and joy.

The prophet Amos talks about the Lord restoring the years that the locusts have eaten. This promise is now true for Naomi. What she lost has been restored. Her "bitterness" has been replaced by "contentment."

The Lord's Plan Unfolds

Through difficulty and tragedy, God brings happiness and fulfillment. Yet He has greater plans that materialize in the future, because they were faithful to His ways.

God's promises

In the Ten Commandments of the Torah, God promises to bless His people.

> For I, the Lord your God, am a jealous God, punishing the children for the sin of the fathers to the third and fourth generation of those who hate me, but showing love to a thousand generations of those who love me and keep My commands.
> —Exodus 20:5–6

Confirmation

Modern sociologists, psychologists and doctors have discovered that the problems of parents are commonly passed on to their children and grandchildren. For example, children of alcoholics are much more likely to become alcoholic, though they've suffered the consequences. Children of abusive parents often become abusive themselves. Many diseases are passed through the genes from one generation to the next.

This is part of what God declares here: Sins of the parents are passed on to the children. It is sad to see our children with the same problems we had, because we know the consequences that follow. We had hoped better for them.

1,000 generations

On the positive side, God also promises to bless those who love and follow Him to a thousand generations. That's a long time.

Archeologists estimate that modern civilizations have been on this planet for less than 10,000 years. Many estimate a generation at forty years, based on the death of the Israelite generation in the wilderness. Thus civilized man has been on this plant for only 250 generations.

So, God promises to bless the descendants of those who love him for 1,000 generations. That is four times longer than the existence of civilized mankind. This is an awesome promise.

Ruth and Boaz didn't consider themselves important or royalty. They were honest people who feared God and kept His ways. Consequently, God blessed their lives. The greater blessings came generations later, after they had died. Their descendents became royalty. The blessings started with their son.

God's Blessing (verse 17b)

And they named him Obed.

The name Obed means "worship." This particular word means "worship by performing acts of service to God."

Remember the beginning of this story, when "my God is king" married "my contentment?" They had two children: "pining away" and "dissipation."

Now we have another marriage, "in Him is strength" marries "friendship;" they have a child called "worship." This romance honors and respects the Lord God, Who orchestrated this marriage through the willingness and faithfulness of Ruth and Boaz.

God's Plan (verse 17c)

He was the father of Jesse, the father of David.

The Lord was not only dealing with Naomi, Boaz, and Ruth, He was planning three generations later for a man named David, who would establish Israel's royal line.

The greatness of King David came from his great grandparents: Boaz, son of Rahab, who lived a life of honor and reputation, and Ruth, a Moabitess, who lived a life of devotion and commitment. Ruth's devotion became David's strength, for he was known as "a man after God's own heart."

THE FAMILY TREE

This story ends much the same way it began: with a family tree. The first family tree was of one man and his immediate family. This family tree covers nine generations. It is the greater picture into which our story fits.

In those days genealogies were part of one's identity—who you are. They also provided back up in a weakly controlled society. Family provided protection, provision and support. This is an influential family in the royal line of the tribe of Judah.

The Progenitors (verse 18–21a)

These then are the descendants of Perez:
Perez fathered Hezron,
Hezron fathered Ram,
Ram fathered Aminadab,
Aminadab fathered Nahshon,
Nahshon fathered Salmon,
Salmon fathered Boaz,

These are the men of the royal line of Judah. Perez is the son of Judah by Tamar. He is the father of the half of the royal line that resided in Bethlehem of Judah.

Salmon was leader of the tribe of Judah when Israel left the wilderness to begin the conquest of Canaan under Joshua. Perhaps he was one of the two spies who went to Jericho and was hidden by Rahab. These spies also rescued her and her family when Israel conquered Jericho. We do know that Salmon married Rahab and fathered Boaz by her.

Details of these other lives are not mentioned, so we don't know their stories. Perhaps some were as poignant as that of Boaz and Ruth. Scripture has given us insight only into this cameo of early, royal Jewish history.

Our Heroes (verse 21b)

Boaz fathered Obed,

Boaz is a man of reputation, affluence, and character. He waited patiently until later in life to find the woman God had arranged for him. She had equal character, beauty, and friendliness. Their son is named "worship," which means worship in serving God. It is an apt epitaph on their lives.

Obed is raised by his grandmother, parents and people devoted to following the Lord. This is a magnificent heritage for himself and his descendants.

Their Descendants (verse 22)

Obed fathered Jesse, and Jesse fathered David.

This is an incredible lineage. These are the parents of King David, Israel's greatest king. This is the David who killed Goliath, conquered all Israel's enemies, and established Israel's greatest dynasty. His kingdom remained intact, ruled by his descendants, for more than 400 years.

David's Character and Life

King David's most outstanding character trait was his devotion to God, which is why he is called "a man after God's own heart."

I suggest that his devotion came from his great grandmother, Ruth, who clung to her mother-in-law Naomi, and said,

> Where you go I will go, and where you stay I will stay. Your people will be my people and your God my God. Where you die I will die, and there I will be buried. May the Lord deal with me, be it ever so severely, if anything but death separates you and me.
> —Ruth 1:16–17

Ruth lived up to those words and commitment. Her life demonstrates faithfulness to God and His ways.

David displayed this same devotion to following the Lord. For years he ran from Saul in the wilderness and deserts of Israel, running and hiding for his life. Again and again he relied on the Lord. The Lord was faithful to rescue and keep him safe.

David gained God's favor. He eventually became king, ruling Judah and all Israel for forty years. He lived to see his son Solomon succeed him on the throne, and died peacefully in his old age.

David's Poetry

David writes about his relationship to God in the Psalms, which became the hymns of the ancient Israelites. Two psalms serve as examples of how David expresses his devotion to God:

> The Lord is my light and my salvation—whom shall I fear?
> The Lord is the stronghold of my life—of whom shall I be afraid?

The Blessings of Following God

When evil men advance against me to devour my flesh,
when my enemies and my foes attack me, they will stumble and fall.
Though an army besiege me, my heart will not fear;
though war break out against me, even then will I be confident.

One thing I ask of the Lord, this is what I seek:
that I may dwell in the house of the Lord all the days of my life,
to gaze upon the beauty of the Lord
and to seek Him in His temple.
For in the day of trouble
He will keep me safe in His dwelling;
He will hide me in the shelter of his tabernacle
and set me high upon a rock.

—Psalm 27

The Lord is my Shepherd,
I shall not want.
He makes me lie down in green pastures,
He leads me beside quiet waters,
He restores my soul.
He guides me in paths of righteousness
For His Name's sake.

Even though I walk
Through the valley
Of the shadow of death,
I will fear no evil,
For You are with me;
Your rod and Your staff,
They comfort me.

You prepare a table before me
In the presence of my enemies.

You anoint my head with oil;
My cup overflows.
Surely goodness and love will follow me
All the days of my life,
And I will dwell in the house of the Lord forever.
—Psalm 23

David's Heritage

There are more than sixty psalms of David recorded in the book of the Psalms as sacred Scripture. They reach from the depths of human despair to the heights of regal victory and always exhort us to follow the Lord. He received this devotion to God from his great grandmother, Ruth, and nourished it to the conclusion of a great and royal life.

The last word in this book is "David." How fitting. I think God brought Ruth, an outsider, to Bethlehem because He wanted her in His family tree. He wanted her to impart her devotion to God to David and his future promised descendent—the Messiah of Israel and the world.

Chapter 8 Spiritual Pearl:

God's ultimate blessings are beyond our comprehension.

CHAPTER NINE

REFLECTIONS ON RUTH

SPIRITUAL PRINCIPLES

Ruth exemplifies character, faithfulness, and devotion to God. Her story challenges us to adopt spiritual values and practice godly living. These values and practices are embraced by civilizations around the world where their religious heritage recognizes a God of justice and grace.

A Dissenting Thought

Unfortunately, many today have given up on ethics. Those values may have worked in the past, they contend, but not today. Today is for the quick and greedy. Success is measured in dollars without sense.

The result is loss in quality of life. We have basic needs in life: food, shelter, and clothing. Once these needs are met, how much more do we need? How much of ourselves do we give up for a little bit more? And when we get more, do we become content?

Measuring Values

You can't measure someone's life at one moment in time. On any given day we encounter obstacles, difficulties, and progress. The real success of one's life can be measured only from within at the end of one's life.

Ruth wasn't famous or royal, simply a woman of character. She endured early tragedy in the death of her husband. Her later rewards were a good husband, a son, and respect.

She was content as she looked back over her life. She had gained God's favor. Fame followed from her descendants, generations after she was gone.

Other Examples

I talked to a man who had built up a respectable estate and then lost it. His comment was, "The money means nothing. I've never been better. I've never had a stronger spiritual relationship with God." He feels more fulfilled living on basics than he did with two homes.

In my own life the greatest rewards have been the lifestyles of my children and the rearing of my grandchildren. Their health and spiritual well-being are worth more than money can buy.

Spiritual Values

I am convinced that the spiritual pearls in each chapter of this book are true. They are part of a belief system and lifestyle that lead to a fulfilling and worthwhile life.

I wrote this book to reflect the life and character of Ruth accurately and clearly. Her life is a poignant testimony to the benefit of spiritual values.

Spiritual Pearls of Ruth:

- Not following God results in disappointment, emptiness, disaster, and sometimes premature death.
- The decision to follow God may be difficult, but it is the only path that leads to hope and fulfillment. It includes adhering to His ways and associating with His people.
- Following God requires character, making the right moral choices in the circumstances of life.
- God rewards faithful character and obedience.
- God's path often presents difficulties that need to be resolved by following God's ways and trusting Him for the best outcome.
- Following God often requires waiting with God in prayer.
- When we follow God through stress and trials, He gives us what is best for us.
- God's ultimate blessings are beyond our comprehension.

To order additional copies of

Ruth

Have your credit card ready and call

Toll free: (877) 421-READ (7323)

or send $8.95 each plus $4.95 S&H* to

WinePress Publishing
PO Box 428
Enumclaw, WA 98022

www.winepresspub.com

*WA residents, add 8.4% sales tax

*add $1.00 S&H for each additional book ordered